# A DUBIOUS HERITAGE

# A Dubious Heritage

*Studies in the Philosophy of Religion
after Kant*

*by*
**Louis Dupré**

**A NEWMAN BOOK**
from
**PAULIST PRESS**
New York/Ramsey/Toronto

Library of Congress
Catalog Card Number: 77-83577

ISBN: 0-8091-2068-2

Published by Paulist Press
*Editorial Office:* 1865 Broadway, New York, N.Y. 10023
*Business Office:* 545 Island Road, Ramsey, N.J. 07446

Printed and bound in the
United States of America

# Contents

INTRODUCTION......................................................................1

### PART I
### THE LEGITIMATION OF RELIGIOUS EXPERIENCE

1. SCHLEIERMACHER'S RELIGION AS FEELING...........9

2. KIERKEGAARD'S RELIGION AS FREEDOM ..............30

3. HEGEL'S RELIGION AS REPRESENTATION...............53

### PART II
### THE SEARCH FOR A METHOD

4. HUSSERL'S INTENTIONS OF EXPERIENCE ..............75

5. BLONDEL'S REFLECTION ON EXPERIENCE..............94

6. DUMÉRY'S REDUCTIONS OF EXPERIENCE.............108

### PART III
### THE JUSTIFICATION OF RELIGIOUS FAITH

7. THE COSMOLOGICAL ARGUMENT ...........................131

8. THE TELEOLOGICAL ARGUMENT ...........................152

9. THE MORAL AND THE
   ONTOLOGICAL ARGUMENTS....................................166

# Introduction

The study of religion did not become a separate branch of philosophy until Kant. Earlier a few attempts had been made to treat religion as a subjective mode of consciousness rather than as a section of metaphysics or ethics. But those approaches mostly resulted from serious doubts about the objective claims of religion in general, or, more specifically, of the Christian revelation. Not surprisingly, its authors reduced faith to a *purely* subjective state of mind that would be dispelled by the Enlightenment. Contrary to such skeptics Kant accepted religion on its own terms. His attempt to define its boundaries in epistemological terms was part of his general plan to submit the entire field of consciousness to a transcendental critique, not in order to undermine its objective claims, but rather to reestablish them as much as possible after the onslaught of Hume's skepticism. Thus *Religion Within the Limits of Reason Alone*, for all its deficiencies, must be read as a thoroughly positive and pioneeringly modern work. Nor is its scope restricted to the immediate concerns of the Enlightenment. It is, in fact, the first methodic effort to formulate and, at the same time, to overcome, the malaise from which the religious consciousness had suffered ever since art, science, philosophy, and morality had become independent of faith. After the spiritual revolution of the Renaissance, religion had become severed from the rest of man's spiritual life. Faith was no longer everything, as it was in the Middle Ages, but *something* and no one seemed to know exactly what. Kant's critical philosophy clearly circumscribed its limits.

It is often said that Kant's philosophy completed the Reformation's turn toward a purely interior religion. But such a statement oversimplifies the matter in more than one way. For Luther himself continued a subjective tradition which Augustine, Anselm and most of the Christian mystics had initiated long before. Also,

1

the priority of the subject in Kant's philosophy cannot be attributed primarily to his religious outlook. It had begun with Descartes' thesis that mind is an entirely unique mode of being which, far from being determined by the nature of non-mental reality, imposes its own determinations upon the definition of nature. Nevertheless, Descartes had kept mind and objective reality separate, as two different substances. With Kant, subjectivity changed from a principle *parallel to* the objective world into a principle *constitutive of* objectivity. Obviously, then, a discussion of transcendence must likewise include an evaluation of the subject's role. It is no secret that that role had received but scant attention from past theologians. Moreover, since knowledge consists essentially in bringing phenomena to objectivity and in reflecting on this process, one can no longer *assume*, as in precritical days, that the mind is adequately equipped to make positive assertions about a transphenomenal reality. Kant's critique of knowledge discredited the traditional "proofs" for the existence of God and gave a whole new direction to the understanding of faith.

Equally momentous was Kant's Copernican revolution in the practical order. If morality is no longer determined by the object of the ethical act but by the subjective intention of the agent, man becomes fully autonomous in the practical as well as in the theoretical order. The religious problems created by Kant's concept of autonomy were balanced by the solutions which his moral philosophy offered elsewhere. In the practical order, Kant saw an opportunity to extend the realm of certainty beyond the rigorous limits which he had set to the domain of objective knowledge. Thus religion's exclusion from scientific knowledge was no ground, as Hume thought, for dismissing it as unworthy of the mature mind. Kant's decision to reintroduce God as a postulate of the moral imperative, and religion as a complement to ethics, may strike us as an unusually narrowing one. It was in fact, a daring attempt to extend the realm of consciousness so as to include legitimately the entire area of religion. Meanwhile it created some problems of its own.

The concept of moral autonomy, on which Kant's ethical system was based, tolerated no transcendent foundation. Kant had defined religion as the recognition of all duties as divine commands, but either this recognition introduces a new element into morality, and then the moral law becomes God's law, thus destroying man's autonomy, or the recognition remains extrinsic to the moral law, and then religion remains without real impact. Kant's solution of this dilemma satisfied no one, not even himself if we may believe his posthumous papers. But at least he had clearly stated a problem which proved to be of vital importance to the philosophy of religion.

Kant's pioneering work resulted in three conclusions which have affected all subsequent philosophy of religion.

1. Since reliable theoretical knowledge is restricted to the objective, phenomenal sphere, the religious consciousness can expect no direct support of its beliefs from theoretical reason.

2. Since the transcendent does not belong to the objective, phenomenal sphere, it must be approached through the subject's awareness of itself rather than through that of its world.

3. Since the subject must be conceived as essentially autonomous, no transcendent reality can ever interfere with the exercise of human freedom.

Each of these conclusions contains a fundamental challenge to all subsequent speculation about religion.

1. How can we restore the theoretical support of religious faith after Kant's critique of the arguments for the existence of God?

2. How can a method be conceived for the philosophical study of religion on the basis of the experience alone?

3. How can that experience itself be legitimated within the context of human autonomy?

Surprisingly, the last challenge was the first one to be met. Two major thinkers took up the question of autonomy shortly after it had been formulated. Schleiermacher linked the problem to the subject-object opposition of cognitive and volitional acts, and showed how feeling overcomes this opposition. Kierkegaard directly took issue with Kant's view of freedom. Autonomous freedom, he claimed, is not an ultimate: it is bound to fail, and in its failure inevitably encounters the question of transcendence.

Kierkegaard wrote, of course, well after Hegel and, to a great extent, against him. Yet as regards Kant's challenge, he dealt with

a more basic matter. For Kant had left no avenue open to the
religious object but that of experience itself. The latter must be justified before the former can properly be discussed. We therefore
thought that Kierkegaard's attempt to legitimate the religious experience should precede Hegel's discussion of its meaning.

Assuming, then, the legitimacy of the religious experience, a
central problem for post-Kantian philosophy became: Which
method allows us to make meaningful statements concerning the
object of the experience *on the sole basis of the experience*? On the
whole, continental philosophy did not give serious attention to the
question until the beginning of this century. Hegel was the brilliant
exception. But most of his predecessors or immediate successors
either ignored the issue and uncritically continued to trust the objectivity of the experience (the Catholic position in the nineteenth
century) or they were satisfied with a purely subjective interpretation of the experience (the liberal Protestant position). Husserl's
sharp distinction between the experience and the object manifested
through the experience, though primarily directed against contemporary psychological theories of logic, went, in fact, to the heart of
the Kantian predicament. Husserl himself was never able to apply
satisfactorily his own theory to the alleged object of religion, and
the essay devoted to him contains little more than the history of
his failures. Yet his successors, especially Scheler, used it to full
advantage.

Struggling with the same Kantian problem Blondel primarily
concentrated on establishing the objective structures of the experience itself, leaving its object largely to faith. According to him,
philosophy of religion must reflect upon the experience in order to
discover its inner logic, its structure and its proper intentionality.
The fundamental Kantian issue of the reality *beyond the experience* remained unsettled. A French philosopher of our own time
has finally attacked it in all its complexity. Henry Duméry combined Blondel's with Husserl's method. Not so much the Husserl
of the *Logical Investigations*, but the later Husserl who by means
of a series of reductions had attempted to reach, through the experience, the transcendental ground of experience. To Duméry the
transcendental reduction stretched to the ultimate limits of its potential, contains the true solution to Kant's problem, because the

religious experience is concerned with the *ground of all experience* more than with a specific "object" of experience. It also offered untapped resources for justifying the religious attitude in the face of the new challenge of human autonomy presented by Marxist and existentialist philosophers. The believer can concede their claim to an exclusively human responsibility for *all* human values —including scientific categories, aesthetic norms and even religious symbols. For instead of constituting a threat to man's self-determination religion should be seen as the very source of this creativity.

With respect to Kant's first challenge, the invalidation of the traditional arguments for the existence of God, the situation appears quite complex. For this is the one that later philosophers have most consistently recognized, with which they have most tenaciously struggled and which, in my opinion, they have least succeeded in meeting. Speculative efforts, to restore the support of theoretical reason to the assertions of a transcendent reality, have, as we shall see in the third part, forced critical philosophy to qualify a number of allegations against the arguments. Yet, on the whole, they have failed to regain for them their previous authority. What has emerged out of those attempts, however, is a new awareness of the original significance of the arguments.

The essays which appear here have been written over a period of a decade, with no preconceived plan in mind. Yet they all originated from the same concern with the impact of Kant's critique upon the study of religion. I therefore felt justified in collecting them in a more unified context. Most of them have appeared in slightly different form in various journals. I thank the publishers for allowing me to present them here in their natural habitat.

Yale University
Easter 1977

# Part I
# The Legitimation of
# Religious Experience

# 1
# Schleiermacher's Religion as Feeling

The problem of human autonomy which Schleiermacher inherited had grown considerably more threatening to religion since it had first been stated. What Schleiermacher had to cope with was not just Kant's abstract and somewhat empty concept of autonomy, but the concrete ideal of humanistic self-sufficiency of German classicism. Goethe's work epitomizes the Promethean attempt to create a cultural universe which would absorb transcendence itself to a point where the very distinction between immanent and transcendent ceased to make sense. The grinning skepticism of the old rationalists was relatively harmless in comparison with the pagan vitality of Kant's red-blooded successors. It was to those "cultured despisers" of religion, with their superhuman ideal of man, that Schleiermacher addressed *On Religion*. The enemy he challenged was not rationalism, but humanism, a humanism more presumptuous than anything we know today. To complete the challenge: Schleiermacher himself sympathized with the adversary. He fully shared the aspirations of his fellow Romantics and radicalized the principle of autonomy. Kant's attitude toward his own principle had been halfhearted; he lacked the courage to apply it consistently whenever religion was at stake. Schleiermacher, on the contrary, felt that religion had nothing to fear from ethical humanism. His philosophy pretended to escape the Kantian dilemma of either religion or autonomy.

Schleiermacher points out that it is inconsistent with the principle of autonomy to postulate God as a necessity of practical reason. Kant needs God to transform, in the afterlife, man's worthiness-to-be-happy, the result of his moral striving, into actual (i.e., empirical) happiness, a happiness which the opposition between freedom and a deterministic, empirical world prevents him

9

from ever attaining in this life. Even if present happiness were attainable, the purity of the ethical obligation would forbid man to pursue it. But, Schleiermacher objects, if virtue is to be its own reward, then the expectation of anything more than the stern satisfaction of having done one's duty will always destroy its purity. "If the desire for happiness is foreign to morality, later happiness can be no more valid than earlier."[1] Consequently, a religion based on empirical considerations of happiness must necessarily jeopardize a morality which wants to be pure (i.e., non-empirical). Kant had banned religion from the realm of speculative reason but, by a strange inconsistency, preserved it as a necessary complement of practical reason. Schleiermacher completes Kant's critique by banning it from the sphere of reason altogether. Instead, he assigns religion to a sphere of consciousness which precedes the specifications of theoretical and practical reason, in which subject and object remain united in an undifferentiated totality. Preceding the more specific dynamisms of cognition or desire, it remains immune to attacks from either side. To avoid all moral and cognitive connotations Schleiermacher defined this sphere of consciousness as *feeling*.

As might have been expected, this definition came immediately under attack. Both philosophers and theologians objected that it reduced religion to an experience completely lacking in objectivity. Schleiermacher's philosophy of religion was, at best, a mere description of psychic states which had no real object. To treat religion as a mere feeling was to abandon from the outset any attempt to discover objective meaning in it.[2]

### Religion as Feeling

Whatever one may think of the appropriateness of the term "feeling" to describe the religious experience, Schleiermacher certainly intends something other than pure subjectivity. Even in the first discourse of *On Religion* feeling appears to be a state that is related to objectivity:

Why do you not regard the religious life itself, and first those pious exaltations of the mind in which all other known activities are set aside or almost suppressed, and the whole soul is dissolved in the immediate feeling of the Infinite and Eternal? In such moments the disposition you pretend to despise *reveals itself* in primordial and visible form.[3]

The expression "reveals itself" implies some sort of meaning and objectivity. It reminds us of the basic thesis of Husserl's Phenomenology, that all acts of consciousness (including feelings) are intentional and imply a subject-object relationship. A closer analysis of the religious experience, as described by Schleiermacher, will show that although *feeling* has a subjective connotation, strictly speaking, it is not more subjective than objective, since it belongs to a stage of consciousness in which subject and object are still basically identical.

For Schleiermacher, as for Kant, full consciousness results from an opposition between subject and object. Yet, in the post-Kantian tradition of Fichte and Schelling, he holds this opposition to be preceded by a moment of identity. This original moment might be described as *pure* consciousness, that is, consciousness before it becomes consciousness *of something*. Although this ground and ultimate condition of consciousness is not conscious itself, it is possible to grasp it in an indirect, reflective way.

You must apprehend a *living movement*. You must know how to listen to yourselves *before* you own consciousness. At least you must be able to reconstruct from your consciousness your own state. What you are to notice is the *rise* of your consciousness and not to reflect upon something already there.[4]

The words "before," "living movement," and "rise of consciousness" in the quoted text clearly indicate that the constitution of full consciousness is a gradual process. In this process the original identity of subject and object breaks up into an opposition in which either the object or the subject becomes predominant. If the object comes to predominate, consciousness develops into cognition; if the subject gets the upper hand, it becomes consciousness of freedom or activity.

Both knowledge and activity are a desire to be identified with the universe through an object. If the power of the object preponderates, if as intuition or feeling, it enters and seeks to draw you into the circle of their existence, it is always a knowledge. If the preponderating power is on your side, so that you give the impress and reflect yourselves in the objects, it is activity in the narrower sense, external working.[5]

Schleiermacher refuses to identify religion with either cognition or activity. Cognition is always cognition of something specific, something determinate, whereas religion appears as an immediate consciousness of totality "of *all* finite things, *in and through the Eternal*." Schleiermacher does not exclude the possibility of a knowledge of God, either as first cause or as object of a revelation, but he does deny that such knowledge has anything to do with the religious experience as such. One might object that his position is abstract, since there can hardly be a religious experience without some knowledge of the supernatural. The experience never falls from the blue sky, but is gradually prepared by and firmly built into a cognitive process. The very fact that people express their religious experiences in theological terms points to the existence of a previous knowledge.

This objection does not really affect Schleiermacher's position. He himself is the first to admit that religion, like any other experience, "never appears pure."[6] Thus, sacred books, which he considers essentially as expressions of profound religious experiences, always include metaphysical and moral teachings. But the problem is neither what prepares the religious experience nor how it is expressed—rather, what its own true nature is. When Schleiermacher claims that speculative knowledge does not belong to the *essence* of the religious phenomenon, he means that the religious attitude is basically different from the speculative. Almost every philosopher uses the idea of God in his speculation, but that does not make him religious. For the philosopher, the idea of God is, at most, the ultimate answer to the enduring questions of the human mind. God is thereby drawn into the immanent circle of the self, and its world; he becomes merely the keystone of an ideological system. The traditional treatments of "natural theology" or "theodicy" are most revealing in this respect. Their purpose is not to obtain a direct insight into the "object" of the religious experience, but to arrive at a coherent interpretation of man and the universe, which, as their authors claim, requires the acceptance of a first cause. Pascal was right in distinguishing the God of Abraham, Isaac, and Jacob from the God of the philosophers. But he might as well have added "the God of the theologians," for the theologian, as much as the philosopher, tries to *understand*, that is, he looks for the rational coherence of what he first accepts as an object of faith. This is not to say that he merely seeks a rational foundation for his faith—he may even reject the possibility of such an attempt—but he wants to understand what that which is beyond reason means to reason. St. Anselm's *fides quaerens intellectum* perfectly expresses the theologian's quest for insight. The religious man, on the contrary, does not try to understand; the purpose of his contemplation is not to obtain more *insight* into the world structure, or even into the object of a supernatural revelation. His contemplation is not immanent, as all rational cognition is; it is an *ek-stasis*, a complete surrender to a totality which transcends the self, although the self is part of it.

This ecstatic character of the religious consciousness becomes even more obvious when we compare it to the moral attitude. Again, Schleiermacher admits that religion has always influenced man's morality, but he insists that the two are essentially different. The moral attitude is always active, the religious is mainly passive:

> While morality always shows itself as manipulating, as self-controlling, piety appears as a surrender, a submission to be moved by the Whole that stands over against man. Morality depends, therefore, entirely on the consciousness of freedom, within the sphere of which all that it produces falls. Piety, on the contrary, is not at all bound to this side of life. In the opposite sphere of necessity, where there is no properly individual action, it is quite as active. Wherefore the two are different.[7]

Schleiermacher does not deny that the surrender of the religious man can to a certain extent be called a moral act (even in his passivity man remains actively responsible), much less that this surrender will affect his whole moral behavior. What he does say is that the religious *attitude* is essentially different from the moral attitude. In morality the idea of God is, at most, the ultimate ground of man's activity, but moral activity, to the extent that it is merely moral, remains self-centered. Even the love of God is pursued as a perfection of one's humanity. Religion, on the contrary, is a search for God not insofar as he is a perfection of my own being, but as he is in himself, that is, insofar as he is transcendent.

Yet, it is not so much Schleiermacher's distinction of religion from speculative knowledge and morality, as his identification of religion with feeling that has been the main object of attacks. For a better understanding of this identification we must return to the dialectic of consciousness. We have already seen that consciousness starts from an undifferentiated unity of subject and object which gradually breaks up as it reaches full consciousness in cognition or activity. But before it becomes either one, consciousness passes through a transitional phase, in which the subject-object equilibrium is not yet destroyed, although it has lost its original purity. There appears a slight differentiation between subject and object, not so pronounced as to result in specific knowledge or activity, but sufficient for creating a vague, highly subjective awareness of self and non-self, not as opposed, but as mutually including each other in one totality. The object—if we may call object what is still indistinct from the subject—is not specified as *this* or *that*. Rather, it is the whole of objectivity as such, out of which particular objects will be born as it further detaches itself from the subject. The subject, likewise, is not yet this particular subject, limited by a world of objects, but subjectivity as such, which, not having freed itself from its embrace of the universe, is still unaware of its individuality. Schleiermacher describes this fleeting moment in the following passage:

> It is the first contact of the universal life with an individual. It fills no time and fashions nothing palpable. It is the holy wedlock of the universe with the incarnated Reason for a creative, productive embrace. It is immediate, raised above all error and misunderstanding. You lie directly on the bosom of the infinite world. In that moment, you are its soul.[8]

Although the identity of subject and object is still preserved, this stage of consciousness already manifests a *more* subjective and a *more* objective aspect. The former we call feeling, the latter intuition. Without this initial differentiation there would be no consciousness at all.

Either the intuition displays itself more vividly and clearly, like the figure of the vanishing mistress to the eyes of her lover; or feeling issues from your heart and overspreads your whole being, as the blush of shame and love over the face of the maiden. At length your consciousness is finally determined as one or the other, as intuition or feeling. Then, even though you have not quite surrendered to this division and lost consciousness of your life as a unity, there remains nothing but the knowledge that they were originally one, that they issued simultaneously from the fundamental relation of your nature.[9]

Feeling and intuition are still predominantly identical, but in feeling this identity is seen from the point of view of the subject, whereas in intuition it is seen from the point of view of the object. One cannot exist without the other: every feeling is the feeling of an intuition and every intuition is the intuition of a feeling. In the first edition of *On Religion* Schleiermacher was very specific on this point:

Intuition is nothing without feeling: it has neither the right origin nor the right force—nor is feeling anything without intuition. Both are real only when and because they are originally one and unseparated.[10]

The religious experience lies in this second moment of consciousness: it is a feeling and intuition of the individual's identity with the All. Clearly, the religious consciousness can never be pure, for as soon as we become aware of this identity it is already breaking up. In a sense, then, religion is nothing but a constant inward movement of consciousness, a continuous search of interiority. This interiority, however, should not be confused with immanence, for it is precisely in the interiority of consciousness that we become aware of the transcendent.

Unfortunately, after the first edition of *On Religion* Schleiermacher uses only the term "feeling" to describe the religious experience. "Intuition" is dropped, either because of the aesthetic connotations which it had with Schlegel or because of its idealistic overtones in Schelling's philosophy. As a result, many commentators have failed to see that the religious experience is just as objective as it is subjective, and have interpreted it as an entirely subjective state not basically distinct from an emotion. But whether Schleiermacher uses the more objective term "intuition" or the more subjective "feeling" to describe the pre-reflective state of consciousness is not very important, since feeling and intuition are not opposed to each other. They are two aspects of one and the same experience. Schleiermacher himself repeatedly refers to an objective aspect, the revelation, which the religious feeling necessarily implies. In *The Christian Faith* he uses the more appropriate term "immediate consciousness," but, lest he appear to have changed his ideas, adds that this expression is equivalent to "feeling."[11]

Let us now see how Schleiermacher identifies this pre-reflective consciousness with the religious experience. Since he takes this identity more or less for granted in *On Religion*, we must use the more detailed analysis which he gives in his later works, particularly in *The Christian Faith*, even though his ideas in the meantime may have undergone a slight evolution.

He carefully distinguishes the *immediate* self-consciousness from what is usually understood by self-consciousness (i.e., a representation of oneself mediated by self-contemplation) and which belongs to the objective order, the order of cognition.[12] The immediate self-consciousness is the transcendent ground of consciousness in which the objective and the subjective orders, the orders of thinking and of willing, coincide. It is neither the being of the object which in thinking is posited in the subject, nor the being of the subject which in willing is posited in the object, but the *positing being* itself. The reflective consciousness becomes aware of this immediate consciousness in its transition from thinking to willing and from willing to thinking.[13]

Yet this transition is not the only moment in which consciousness is immediate. At any moment both thinking and willing preserve a connection with their common origin, and feeling accompanies each moment of the reflective consciousness.

To the extent that thinking is also willing and vice versa, the immediate consciousness must be present at every moment. We thus find feeling steadily accompanying each moment, be it predominantly thinking or willing. It seems to vanish when we are totally absorbed in an intuition[14] or in an activity. But this only seems so. Yet, at the same time, it always merely accompanies. Sometimes it seems to present itself alone, submerging all thought or activity. But this again is a mere semblance, for with it vestiges of willing and germs of thought, or vice versa, are always given, however faintly.[15]

Every self-consciousness now contains two basic elements: a more active, which accounts for the identity of the self *(ein Sichselbstsetzen)*, and a more passive, in which the variability of the self's state of being is founded *(ein Sichselbstnichtsogesetzthaben)*.

The latter of these presupposes for every self-consciousness another factor besides the Ego, a factor which is the source of the particular determination, and without which the self-consciousness would not be precisely what it is. *But this Other is not objectively presented in the immediate self-consciousness* with which alone we are here concerned. For though, of course, the double constitution of self-consciousness causes us always to look objectively for an Other to which we can trace the origin of our particular state, yet this search is a separate act with which we are not at present concerned.[16]

The active and passive elements appear already in the pre-reflective, the immediate stage of self-consciousness. Schleiermacher defines the active element on the immediate level as *feeling of freedom*, the receptive element as *feeling of dependence*. The feeling of freedom can never be absolute, for free action always refers to an object which has somehow been given and presupposes a certain receptivity on the part of the subject. Not only is the subject through its activity unable to make an object come altogether into existence, but the existence of the subject itself is immediately perceived as passive "because our whole existence does not present itself to our consciousness as having proceeded from our own spontaneous activity."[17] Consequently, in a temporal existence there can be no feeling of absolute freedom.

The same holds true for the feeling of absolute dependence with respect to any particular object: No object can impose itself so absolutely that the self can have no free counter influence upon it. Even the totality of this world cannot account for a feeling of *absolute* dependence, since there always remains the possibility that man exercises influence on all its parts. However, the immediate *self-consciousness* which accompanies every particular activity and which excludes a feeling of absolute freedom, is a consciousness of *absolute* dependence, for it results from the awareness "that the whole of our spontaneous activity comes from a source outside of us in just the same sense in which anything towards which we should have a feeling of absolute freedom must have proceeded entirely from ourselves."[18] Schleiermacher then identifies this feeling of absolute dependence with religion.

At this point the reader might raise the difficulty: How can there be a *feeling* (i.e., an immediate consciousness) of dependence, and, even more, a *feeling* of freedom? Freedom is in the reflective consciousness, as we already know from *On Religion*, and dependence seems to require an object on which one depends, which likewise exists only in reflection. It would appear, therefore, that the words "dependence" and "freedom" are entirely out of place in the immediate self-consciousness. The objection is substantial and I do not try to minimize it. Yet, it seems to me that the combination of "feeling" and "freedom" is not contradictory. For Schleiermacher's feeling of freedom is not a full-fledged consciousness of freedom, which would indeed require a subject-object opposition. Rather, it refers to a moment of the immediate consciousness which is *leading to* the reflective consciousness of freedom. Such feeling is by no means contradictory, for we know that even the immediate consciousness has already a certain differentiation, without which it would not be consciousness at all. It is, so to speak, on its way to becoming full consciousness, and the direction which it has taken shows from the very beginning.

To understand this, the reader should keep in mind that feeling is both one and manifold. It is one, insofar as the subject is not yet specified by any particular object: there is no object, but only the totality of all possible objects. It is manifold, insofar as the subject can be present in this totality in various ways. This variety results from the fact mentioned above, that even the immediate consciousness must have some specification if there is to be consciousness at all. The specification comes not from a fully determinate object (the object of reflective consciousness) but from the objective *totality already on its way* to becoming this or that object. In its purity, then, feeling would be absolutely *one*, without any specification whatever. But this pure feeling never exists. When we become conscious of it, the one feeling has already taken on certain determinations, which accounts for the many shades we distinguish in it.[19] On the basis of the subject's initial attitude toward an object which as yet is not constituted, Schleiermacher distinguishes the feeling of freedom from the feeling of dependence. These two basic feelings inaugurate, on a pre-reflective level, the distinction between consciousness of freedom and consciousness of necessity.

*Feeling and Reflection*

Yet, one might ask, how is this interpretation compatible with Schleiermacher's theory that a feeling of freedom or dependence "accompanies" man's reflectively conscious activity? We have shown the immediate consciousness of feeling to be a *transition* between the original subject-object identity and the reflective consciousness. It is, therefore, not only clearly distinct from the reflective, but always on its way to becoming reflective. How, then, can it maintain itself simultaneously with the reflective consciousness? The answer is that feeling, by its very nature, can never exist alone, but must necessarily accompany reflective consciousness. As soon as we try to live a feeling in itself, it becomes something else. The moment we concentrate on it, it ceases to be feeling and becomes reflection; the immediate consciousness can never be brought into focus without becoming objective. The images by which Schleiermacher describes the religious feeling on pages 43-44 of *On Religion* (from which we quoted above) strongly emphasize its vanishing character. He calls it "scarcely in time at all, so swiftly it passes," "fleeting and transparent as the vapour which the dew breathes on blossom and fruit," "like the figure of the vanishing mistress to the eyes of her lover."

A feeling can survive only by avoiding the spotlight of reflection, that is, by *accompanying* another act which itself is reflective. It can be consciously present only as a sort of background music in the midst of thinking and internal activity. All our attention is focused on the thought or activity, and yet we are aware of feelings all the time. We become fully conscious of them only when we reflect upon them, and then they disappear. But the very fact that we are able to reflect upon them and to catch their most subtle shades and changes, even when they are no longer present, shows that, in a non-reflective way, we were very much conscious of them. There is, then, no contradiction in Schleiermacher's theory of the simultaneous presence of the immediate and the reflective consciousness, because they are present in a different way.

Nor has Schleiermacher abandoned his position that in feeling there is no explicit subject-object opposition. A feeling is not an attitude one takes vis-à-vis the universe, but a certain mode of being-with-the-universe. No sharp distinction between the two is possible at this level. Schleiermacher's feelings of freedom and dependence are an active and a passive being-with-the-universe. Neither of these feelings reveals the universe as an *object*, over which I have power or which has power over me. There is no *object*, in the strict sense of the word, in feeling; there is only the being-in-a-certain-situation which has a more objective and a more subjective aspect. It is precisely for that reason that Schleiermacher in the above-quoted text (p. 104) drew such a sharp distinction between the feeling of dependence and the *consciousness of the Other* as objectively presented. The *feeling* of dependence knows no Other, any more than it knows a self.

But this very distinction has led to another difficulty, for it would seem that religion always presupposes an Other in the objective sense, a presupposition which Schleiermacher has carefully excluded from the religious experience. How can there be religion without some *concept* of God? Schleiermacher answers that "God" originally is not a concept, but merely an expression of the feeling of absolute dependence. Whether one has a *concept* of God or not is entirely irrelevant to the religious experience as such. Man invented a special word for God not in order to designate a new object of knowledge, but to express a feeling which goes beyond all objects. It would even be wrong to say that God (i.e., the feeling of absolute dependence) is *given* to me in an original revelation. For if God were *given*, he would become an object, and thus subject to my counter influence. I could accept him or reject him. But in that case the term "God" would no longer refer to a feeling of *absolute* dependence.

Schleiermacher fully admits that God will necessarily become an objective concept, a symbolic expression. But as such it is altogether distinct from the original feeling, which is never objective. If one does not keep this distinction in mind, the symbolic expression will betray the original experience: "The transference of the idea of God to any perceptible object, unless one is all the time conscious that it is a piece of purely arbitrary symbolism, is always a corruption, whether it be a temporary transference, i.e., a theophany, or a constitutive transference, in which God is represented as permanently a particular perceptible existence."[20]

But if Schleiermacher's theory of feeling is coherent, the basic question still remains: What made him consider feeling to be the essence of the religious experience? The answer lies in the fact that the feeling of dependence reveals the transcendent ground of self-consciousness, the point where consciousness is no longer opposed to, but coincides with, reality. Feeling alone suppresses all opposition within consciousness and, therefore, also the opposition with the other-than-consciousness. It unites consciousness with all being.

This transcendent determination of self-consciousness is its religious aspect, or the *religious feeling*, and in it the transcendent ground or the supreme being is itself presented. It is present, then, insofar as in our self-consciousness is also posited the reality of all things as active and passive (as in our own case), that is, insofar as we identify ourselves with the reality of all things and they with us. It is present as condition of all being, which is woven into the opposition of receptivity and self-activity, *i.e., as universal feeling of dependence.*[21]

This difficult text shows that, in the final analysis, Schleiermacher is looking for a manifestation of Kant's ultimate unconditioned condition or Schelling's absolute ground or Hegel's identity of the ideal and the real. He finds such manifestation in feeling, because in this privileged moment consciousness reaches the complete *coincidentia oppositorum.* It follows, then, that religion for Schleiermacher is not merely a subjective experience, as many people have thought, but a revelation of the ultimate ground of reality and consciousness. Like Kant, Fichte, and Schelling, Schleiermacher is looking for the *absolute,* not for a sentimental experience; and whatever moment of consciousness reveals the absolute, he will call religion. Even though the immediate consciousness has no object, as thinking and willing do, it still has an intentionality of its own, for it reveals the subject-object totality. This aspect of revelation was always present in the notion of feeling: we found it in the first discourse of *On Religion,*[22] and we still find it in the *Dialektik.*

My interpretation is confirmed by an important passage in *The Christian Faith,* where Schleiermacher claims that not all feelings are religious, but only the "highest grade of immediate self-consciousness,"[23] that is, the feeling of absolute dependence. The immediate self-consciousness also has a lower form, which connects it with perceptible finite existence and which splits up into a partial feeling of dependence and a partial feeling of freedom. This might easily have led to inconsistencies, for, as we saw before, feeling is essentially one. But Schleiermacher adds that the immediate self-consciousness combines the different moments into a stable unity. The feeling of absolute dependence, if present, structures the lower moments of feeling into a synthesis of which it is the determining factor: "This relatedness of the sensibly determined to the higher self-consciousness in the unity of the moment is the consummating point of the self-consciousness."[24]

The feelings of partial dependence and partial freedom are necessary to make the feeling of absolute dependence come into consciousness at all, that is, to make it into a determinate feeling, but they do not constitute the religious consciousness as such. They only make it into *this* or *that* particular religious feeling.

> Being related as a constituent factor to a given moment of consciousness which consists of a partial feeling of freedom and a partial feeling of dependence, it (i.e., the religious consciousness) thereby becomes a particular religious emotion, and being in another moment related to a different datum, it becomes a different religious emotion; yet so that the essential element, namely, the feeling of absolute dependence, is the same in both, and thus throughout the whole series, and the difference arises simply from the fact that it becomes a different moment when it goes along with a different determination of the sensible self-consciousness.[25]

We may conclude, then, that the religious consciousness does not coincide with the entire immediate consciousness, but is only one moment of it. Only as feeling of absolute dependence does feeling reveal the absolute. This qualification proves that Schleiermacher is more interested in what the experience reveals (its intuition) than in its subjective aspect.

A similar impression is conveyed by Schleiermacher's remark in the *Dialektik* that the religious experience is never pure. This statement is meaningless if we take it to be a judgment on the experience itself rather than on what it reveals, since the experience *qua* experience lacks any objective standard and does not admit of degrees of purity. However, if we compare the experience to its intuition, that is, to the transcendent ground of being in which all oppositions cease to exist, then it is correct to say that the actual experience always falls short, for it is never able to rid itself completely of all oppositions. "Although the religious feeling is really achieved, it is never pure, because the consciousness of God in it always implies otherness" *(das Bewusstsein Gottes ist darin immer an einem anderen).*[26]

Schleiermacher's theory that in the feeling of absolute dependence the transcendent ground of being and consciousness reveals itself, reminds one of Karl Jaspers' philosophy. Like Jaspers,

Schleiermacher considers the revelation of the transcendent to belong to the essence of human existence. In *The Christian Faith* he writes: "If the feeling of absolute dependence expressing itself as consciousness of God, is the highest grade of immediate self-consciousness, it is also an essential element of human nature."[27] Several other similarities between Schleiermacher's feeling of absolute dependence and Jaspers' existential relation to the transcendent have been pointed out.[28] But Jaspers would never call this existential experience of the transcendent a *feeling*.

## The Aesthetic and the Religious Experience

All these facts, particularly the distinction of religion from all other feelings, and the search for an ever greater interiority, make one wonder whether the term "feeling," with its connotation of an effortless, half-dreaming state of mind, correctly describes what Schleiermacher intends. Yet, in spite of these intrinsic difficulties and growing criticism from without, Schleiermacher persisted in using a term by which we normally refer to the aesthetic experience. This is probably due to the fact that Schleiermacher did not clearly perceive the distinction between the religious experience and aesthetic feeling. In *On Religion* he is very articulate in refuting any identification of religion with morality or speculative knowledge, but he becomes extremely vague on the relation between religion and aesthetic feelings and is unable to support his distinction of the sense of beauty from the sense of God by any conclusive proof.[29]

In Schleiermacher's defense we must say that the aesthetic and the religious experiences are closely related and have much more in common than many theologians and philosophers of religion are willing to admit.[30] First of all, like the aesthetic feeling, the religious experience is clearly distinct from speculative knowledge and moral striving. As *On Religion* shows so well, to *think* God is not religion, but philosophy or theology. Likewise, to strive for moral perfection, even if this includes a certain relation to God and a religious sanction, is only indirectly related to the unique apprehension of the transcendent which we call the religious experience. But there is more. In the religious act we find the same equilibrium of the objective and the subjective which characterizes the aesthetic feeling. The religious consciousness transcends every specific theoretical and practical orientation: It unites the knowledge and love of God in *one act* of cognitive surrender.

Furthermore, the aesthetic and the religious experiences are both essentially symbolic. In the aesthetic intuition, the active and passive powers of the mind reach a precarious equilibrium in the loving contemplation of a sensuous image charged with a spiritual content. Something similar happens in the religious act: it, too, is an expression of the mind in its totality, subjective and objective, sensuous and spiritual. That is why man, in his religious life, necessarily creates symbols, that is, sensuous forms laden with spiritual meaning.

But the function of these symbols is entirely different from that of the image in the aesthetic intuition. For the immediate consciousness, the aesthetic image is the adequate representation of a spiritual element, an idea. In aesthetic contemplation, idea and image are so closely joined together that there can be no idea apart from the image. To ask for the *meaning* of a work of art, as if some purely spiritual idea were hidden behind the perceptible form, is a meaningless question. A true work of art is not a surrogate for a philosophical treatise; its meaning lies entirely *in* its appearance, that is, in what we see, hear, and feel. In religion, however, the spirit feels not quite at home in its sensuous forms.

> Nothing is more alien to the image or representational moment of the religious act than this complacent acquiescence (of the aesthetic experience). For the religious act is essentially an attempt to grasp the imageless meaning of the image.[31]

It thus continuously transcends its images in trying to become pure, that is, imageless, contemplation. We might say that the image is there only as a temporary, yet necessary, counterpart of an idea striving to free itself from all limiting determinations.

This intrinsic dynamism gives the religious act a certain dichotomy: it expresses itself in a sensuous form, but at the same time it tries to break through the form. The form itself shows the same ambiguity. On the one hand it rests in its own sensuous-spiritual meaning (as in the aesthetic experience), but on the other hand it signifies a content which entirely transcends this meaning. The symbolism of religious forms is, therefore, more complex than that of aesthetic images, for they intend something over and above their own intrinsic meaning. This double meaning of the religious form has been aptly described as the twofold *noëma* of the religious act.[32]

From its essential shortcoming in the expression of an ever transcendent idea the religious symbol acquires a certain freedom with respect to this idea. The connection between idea and symbol is much looser in the religious act than in the aesthetic experience. That is why the understanding of religious symbols, unlike aesthetic images, always requires an initiation; to the outsider they appear merely as odd signs devoid of meaning. Schleiermacher is well aware of this fact when he writes that the symbolic expression of the religious feeling is always arbitrary.[33]

Unfortunately, he does not draw the conclusions implied in this view. He fails to see how the very distance between the religious experience and its symbolic expression indicates an intrinsic necessity for reflection. The reason why the act cannot be expressed adequately is that it breaks through the immediacy which ties it to a finite determination, and that it tends to become reflective. In transcending its symbols the religious act goes beyond the harmonious but self-complacent equilibrium of aesthetic contemplation. This does not exclude the existence of a religious feeling. But as mere *feeling* this religiously colored experience belongs mainly to the aesthetic order and should therefore be called "religiosity" rather than "religion." It merely initiates an act whose internal dynamism leads beyond the immediacy of feeling, into the realm of reflection.

The same is true for the religious intuition. Although it is originally nothing else than the more objective side of a feeling from which it can hardly be distinguished, it soon tends to detach itself from the subject and to become "another." Yet it never reaches that point, for, as Schleiermacher has clearly seen, as an object opposed to a subject, it would necessarily be finite and thus lose its absolute character. The religious act, therefore, can have no object in the strict sense of the word. However, the reason for this is not, as Schleiermacher thought, that the religious consciousness does not seek reflectivity, but rather that the infinite character of its intuition prevents it from ever becoming an object, and that, therefore, the process of reflection never comes to an end. Here again, we are faced with the ambiguity of the religious act. Even more than cognitive reflection, it attempts to abandon its own subjectivity in an ecstatic effort to reach a term which entirely transcends the self (God is the wholly Other—the *mysterium tremendum*), and, at the same time, it returns into itself, knowing that this term cannot lie outside the subject, for then it would be merely a finite object opposed to a finite subject (God, therefore is immanent—the *mysterium fascinans*). The religious act is thus both an *ekstasis* and an interiorization process. It is both immediate and reflective. Although it continually tends to split up into a subject-object opposition, it never does so.

However, this does not mean, as Schleiermacher claimed, that the religious act never leaves the pre-reflective stage of consciousness. On the contrary, the immediacy[34] of the act is, as Kierkegaard points out, not pre- but *post*-reflective. It moves in a constant dialectic from immediacy to reflection and back to immediacy. Besides this dialectical unrest, the religious immediacy shows another feature that belongs to the reflective consciousness. Unlike the simple apprehension of the aesthetic experience,[35] it always includes an existential judgment concerning the absolute. This existential affirmation would posit the absolute as object were it not immediately corrected by a counter movement identifying the absolute with the subject.

The reflective character of the religious act is further manifested in its tendency to split up into a cognitive act (faith) and a practical act of striving (love). Yet faith is never cognition, and love of God is never striving. The nature of the religious act does not allow a full specification into cognition and striving, since this would result in a subject-object opposition destroying its fundamental unity. Faith and the love of God, therefore, are not basically distinct; one always implies the other.

Schleiermacher struggled long with this problem and vaguely perceived its solution. He clearly saw that the religious act is closely related to the aesthetic experience in that both belong to the immediate consciousness, where subject and object are basically identical. To a certain extent he also saw their difference, as is shown by his distinction between the religious and other feelings, as well as by his emphasis on the former's purity and hidden interiority. Yet he could never admit that a reflective dynamism is inherent in the religious experience and that the experience, in following this dynamism, is intensified rather than destroyed. For him reflection was always equivalent to a subject-object opposition which would necessarily abolish the absolute by making it into "something." As a result, he could no longer adequately distinguish the religious act from aesthetic feeling. Schleiermacher did not see that reflection brings out the intrinsic tension of the religious act but never reduces this act to one of cognition or striving, because the same dynamism which leads religion to reflection also leads it away from the threatening opposition back to the original unity. Without reflection, the infinity of the religious act remains abstract, that is, it is infinite only in the sense that it has never been confronted with the finite (Hegel would call this abstract infinity *die schlechte Unendlichkeit*), and its absolute character remains a mere *appearance* of the absolute, of which one never knows whether subject and object are really identical or whether they merely appear so in the pre-reflective consciousness.

We might conclude, then, that Schleiermacher's basic insight into the nature of religion was correct but that he lacked the philosophical equipment to work it out in a satisfactory way. His great importance consists in having shown that the religious experience is in the very center of human experience, and that a religious determination is therefore essential to human existence.

## NOTES

1. *On Religion*, trans. John Oman (New York, 1958), p. 20. This translation is based on the third edition of *Über die Religion: Reden an die Gebildeten unter ihren Verächtern* (Berlin, 1878).
2. See Emil Brunner, *Die Mystik und das Wort* (Tübingen, 1924).
3. *On Religion*, pp. 15-16. (My italics.)
4. *Ibid.*, p. 41. (My italics.)
5. *Ibid.*, p. 44.

6. *Ibid.*, p. 33.
7. *Ibid.*, p. 37.
8. *Ibid.*, p. 43.
9. *Ibid.*, p. 44.
10. *Über die Religion: Reden an die Gebildeten unter ihren Verächtern*, Neu herausgegeben von Rudolf Otto (Göttingen, 1926), p. 49.
11. *The Christian Faith*, trans. H. R. Mackintosh and J. S. Steward (Edinburgh, 1928), p. 6. *The Christian Faith* is a translation of *Der Christliche Glaube, nach den Grundsätzen der Evangelischen Kirche* (Berlin, 1842).
12. *Ibid.*, p. 6.
13. *Dialektik* (Berlin, 1839), p. 429.
14. "Intuition" here stands for a cognitive act of the reflective consciousness.
15. *Dialektik*, p. 429. (My translation.)
16. *The Christian Faith*, p. 13.
17. *Ibid.*, p. 16.
18. *Ibid.*, p. 16.
19. See L. Vander Kerken, *Religieus Gevoel en Aesthetisch Ervaren* (Antwerp, 1945), pp. 33-34.
20. *The Christian Faith*, p. 18.
21. *Dialektik*, p. 430.
22. See n. 4.
23. *The Christian Faith*, p. 18.
24. *Ibid.*, p. 21.
25. *Ibid.*, pp. 22-23.
26. *Dialektik*, p. 152.
27. *The Christian Faith*, p. 26.
28. See G. J. Hoenderdaal, *Religieuze Existentie en Aesthetische Aanschouwing* (Arnhem, 1943), pp. 54-57; also, P. Jonges, *Schleiermachers Anthropologie* (Groningen, 1942).
29. See, e.g., *On Religion*, pp. 65-67.
30. On the relationship between the religious and the aesthetic experience we have followed the excellent study of L. Vander Kerken, *Religieus Gevoel en Aesthetisch Ervaren*. Although it is probably the best work on this difficult subject, it seems to be completely unknown in Anglo-Saxon countries.
31. Vander Kerken, *op. cit.*, p. 55.
32. *Ibid.*, p. 49.
33. See *The Christian Faith*, p. 18.
34. By "immediacy" we understand, with Schleiermacher and Hegel, a moment of consciousness in which subject and object are not opposed to each other.
35. See "The Analytic of the Beautiful" in Kant's *Critique of Judgment*.

# 2
# Kierkegaard's Religion as Freedom

Man is not free to be free—he *finds* himself to be free. This factual character of freedom raises the question: What is the ground of the free self? Must one accept it as an ultimate fact which allows no further exploration, or does it have its origin in a transcendent source by which freedom is being *given*? Some existentialist philosophers have opted for the first alternative. But their choice leaves unanswered the question why the fact of freedom alone should remain unexamined by philosophy. Søren Kierkegaard radically chose the second alternative and defined the self as a *relation to the transcendent*.[1] With him philosophy becomes essentially *religious*. Undoubtedly, such a theonomic position presents serious problems to a theory which defines the self as freedom. No one was more aware of them than Kierkegaard himself who devoted the entire philosophical part of his *oeuvre* to the solution of the difficulties inherent in his initial position.[2] Indeed, one could describe Kierkegaard's philosophy as a dialectic between the autonomy, implied in the free choice by which the self is constituted, and the theonomy which follows from the fact that this choice is ultimately an acceptance of the self's ontological dependence.

## The Self as Free Choice

Even in Kierkegaard's early writings the realization of the self takes place within a total *givenness* from which freedom itself takes its origin, and which is to be included in the ultimate, existential choice. The second part of *Either/Or* shows how the "aesthetic" attitude tries to escape the limitation, and thereby also the constitution, of the self, by a constant rejection of any commitment. The "aesthete" has no self: his entire existence consists in a variety of experiences determined by outside conditions. The frustration which springs from the refusal of the spirit to found itself results in a strange oppressive melancholy. It would lead to despair were it not that real despair is already an existential choice. Indeed, one does not fall into despair; one freely chooses it and in choosing it, one chooses oneself, since the object of despair is never a particular situation (as the loss of one's fortune or of a beloved being), but oneself *in* a particular situation. He who refuses to commit himself will eventually be confronted with the almost unavoidable choice of accepting or not accepting himself in this frustrated situation. But he will still have to make the choice by an active decision. If he makes it, he posits an absolute in the drifting relativity of his existence and this absolute is precisely what the self is.

The paradox of this absolute self is that it is at once chosen and given. The choice constitutes the absolute, but there can be no absolute choice unless there is already an absolute to be chosen.

> In despair I choose the absolute, for I myself am the absolute,
> I posit the absolute and I myself am the absolute, but in
> complete identity with this I can say that I choose the abso-
> lute which chooses me, that I posit the absolute which posits
> me.[3]

A self which posits itself by choosing itself and which, on the other hand, could not choose itself without preexisting its own choice, must be a free self. Indeed, freedom becomes free only when it asserts itself and yet, how could it assert itself were it not already free?

Not *any* choice of the self, however, posits the self in an absolute way. To choose oneself only within a particular setting of external circumstances is to choose an empirical, relative self. In an absolute choice, on the contrary, a man chooses himself regardless of any circumstances. For that reason we may say that a choice of the authentic self always implies a despair of the relative self, the self in its empirical determinations.

Such an absolute choice of the self makes man into an ethical being, for it alone creates the essential condition for an absolute distinction between good and evil. To posit the self is to posit an absolute good and thus to create an absolute norm for good and evil. "In the fact that I choose the good I make *eo ipso* the choice between good and evil. The original choice is constantly present in every subsequent choice."[4] True enough, speculatively the distinction between good and evil can be understood without any personal commitment. But on the speculative level the distinction remains relative. For pure thought there is no *absolute* contradiction: even if two forms of being contradict each other logically, speculative reason (in Hegel's sense) is always ready to mediate between them, and thus to reconcile them in a higher unity. Only in the actual exercise of freedom does the distinction become absolute, because *lived* freedom posits good and evil in the real order, and that is the only order in which they exclude each other absolutely. "The good *is* for me the fact that I will it, and apart from my willing it, it has no existence. This is the expression for freedom. It is so also with evil, it *is* only when I will it."[5]

The existential choice is absolute only when its object is the self in its totality. But the fact that such an absolute choice is an unqualified good does not imply that every aspect of the self can be indiscriminately approved. Much which man must accept as part of himself is repellent and will in the very act of choosing reveal itself as evil. Yet, if his choice is to be that of a total, concrete self, rather than of a relative, empirical one, it must also include these shadowy aspects of the self. How then can an absolute choice both include and reject the darker elements of the self?

In response to this question, Kierkegaard states that the choice to be absolute and authentic must be a choice in repentance. In repentance alone man is able to express that evil is part of his nature (and therefore to be included in his choice) and, at the same time, that it estranges him from his true nature. A choice of the authentic self must therefore contain a recognition of its imperfection.

Only when I choose myself as guilty do I choose myself absolutely, if any absolute choice of myself is to be made in such a way that it is not identical with creating myself.[6]

By the same token, the choice in repentance implicitly asserts the self's dependence, for in admitting evil to be part of his very nature man affirms its basic givenness. For an absolute choice of the self, the affirmation of the self's dependence is just as necessary as the acceptance of its evil.

But how can the ethical attitude which presupposes an autonomous choice of the self avoid entering into conflict with the acceptance of a transcendental dependence? It is this question which Kierkegaard attempts to answer in *Repetition* and *Fear and Trembling* by showing, dialectically and phenomenologically, how, in its autonomous choice, the self experiences itself as dependent and, also, how the acceptance of this dependence leads it into an entirely new sphere of existence.

## *The Extrinsic Limitation of Freedom: Fate and Necessity*

In *Repetition* Kierkegaard for the first time states the problem which several of his later works try to solve: How can man be free and yet dependent? This philosophical question is hidden beneath a description of the psychological experience of a young man in love who, because of his overly reflective disposition, is unable to realize his love in a permanent union.[7] It has been pointed out that the entire story may be read as Kierkegaard's personal question put to his former fiancee, Regine Olsen: Will I still be able to marry in spite of an emotional attitude incompatible with marriage? Regine's answer came before Kierkegaard was finished with the question. Shortly before the publication of his book, Kierkegaard learned that Regine was engaged and at the last moment he was forced to change the conclusion. These various dimensions of meaning, as well as Kierkegaard's deliberate attempt to lead the uninitiated reader astray, make this seemingly simple story extremely complicated and deceptive.

The basic subject of *The Repetition*, however, is clear enough: it is the tension between freedom and necessity, between self-realization and fate. How can man still be free when destiny prevents him from exercising his freedom? How can freedom overcome the necessity of the unfree, given situation *(Begivenhed)* in which it finds itself? How can man be himself when a higher force hampers his self-determination? How can the self recapture itself after its free realization has been halted by fate?[8]

According to Kierkegaard, philosophy offers no answer to these critically important questions. For the Greek mind the problem of freedom versus destiny did not exist as it does for modern man. Freedom had not yet become fully conscious as a *forward* movement, and philosophical reflection was accordingly confined to a kind of *immediate* consciousness. "The Greeks in a sense were happy; but if their happiness ran out, then recollection appeared as the consolation of freedom: only in recollection and in withdrawal into it did freedom possess eternal life."[9] The recollection of an eternal past was for the Greeks what the self-assertion in a forward leap is to the moderns. "Repetition and recollection are the same movement, only in opposite directions; for what is recollected has been, is repeated backwards, whereas repetition, properly so called, is recollected forwards."[10]

Modern consciousness seeks freedom in the future. Its movement is forward and its eternal possibilities lie in the time to come. But such a leap into the future cannot be understood by philosophy. For philosophy, each moment is already immanently present in the previous one. It is therefore unable to cope with the transcendent leap of freedom. In fact, it is unable to cope with any form of becoming, for becoming is always transcendent to what precedes it: it produces something which was not there before.[11] True enough, by means of mediation Hegel tried to integrate *becoming* in philosophy and even to make it the driving force of his whole system, but in doing so he has merely transformed freedom into necessity, causality into logical ground. "Mediation must be understood in relation to immanence. Thus understood, mediation cannot be employed at all in the sphere of freedom, where the real thing constantly emerges not by virtue of *immanence* but of transcendence."[12] In mediation the actual is *immanent* in the possible, whereas in the movement of freedom, the actual emerges from the possible in a *transcendent* way. The problem of *The Repetition* cannot be stated correctly in the immanent determinations of modern philosophy since these determinations do not allow for true freedom.

The Bible, on the contrary, states the problem very clearly. In the story of Job we perceive the forward impulse of freedom, checked by the intervention of a transcendent power.[13] Job's trial symbolizes the essential difficulty of human freedom. In his failures man experiences the basic insufficiency of the self: the collision between freedom and fate brings him face to face with a force which tramples his freedom. He feels that he is limited and that between himself and the full realization of his self stands the transcendent. Freedom is brought to a sudden halt in its self-conquest by the appearance of a power beyond its control. How can man accept this intrusion of the transcendent without losing his dignity and even his essence as free being?

Two attitudes are possible. One is to resign his autonomous freedom, consider his sufferings a punishment, and renounce the finite for the infinite. This is the attitude commended by Job's friends who try to convince him that he suffers because of his sins. "He knows the false hearts of men, sees wickedness there, and wouldst thou have Him overlook it? . . . thou hast but to cleanse thy hands of their wrong-doing, rid thy dwelling-place of the guilt that defiles it. . . ."[14] This explanation, however, subsumes the transcendent under immanent ethical categories, thus reducing it to a prolongation of the self. God then becomes merely an unpredictable judge of human freedom who takes the place of man's moral responsibility. The arbitrary intervention of such a judge, punishing ethical mistakes which man is unable to avoid or even to recognize as such, makes any responsible free action impossible and debases human dignity. Job refuses to accept this; in spite of his resignation to the transcendent, he firmly upholds the immanent freedom and responsibility of the self.

> As sure as he is a living God, he, the omnipotent, who so refuses me justice, who makes my lot in life so bitter; while life is in me, while he still grants me breath, never shall these lips justify the wrong, never this tongue utter the lie! Gain your point with me you shall not; I will die sooner than abandon my plea of innocence. That claim, once made, I will not forego; not one act in all my life bids my conscience reproach me.[15]

Job's greatness is "that the *passion of freedom* within him is not stifled or tranquilized by a false expression." He maintains that he is right even though the whole world seems to conspire to make him look guilty.

Fate had played him a trick in letting him become guilty. If this is the way it stands, he can never more recapture himself. His nature has become split, and so the question is not about the repetition of something outward, but about the repetition of his freedom.[16]

The loss of his possessions is only a symbol for the split in Job's existence, and their restoration symbolically indicates that his existence, his freedom, has been restored to its integrity *(redintegratio in statum pristinum)*.

Contrary to the attitude of simple resignation, Job takes the transcendent for what it is: an intrusion of the infinite which threatens man's finite existence. Job knows that man has to fight with the transcendent, as Jacob wrestled with Yahweh, if he is to maintain his freedom. He knows that the enemy is not an avenging angel bent on punishing man's ethical shortcomings, but the totally Other before whose transcendence all ethical striving fails, regardless of its immanent righteousness. The immanent and the transcendent are essentially opposed and they cannot be reduced to each other. Nietzsche's attempt to eliminate the transcendent by means of a superhuman immanence has no more foundation in the human condition than the willingness of Job's friends to sacrifice the immanent to the transcendent. Man must simultaneously accept the transcendent in resignation and maintain the rights of the immanent. Job is fully resigned to the loss of his possessions and says: "The Lord hath given; the Lord hath taken away: Blessed be the name of the Lord." Yet, at the same time, he talks back to God and claims his innocence: he may be wrong, but he is wrong only before God—on his own autonomous level he pleads not guilty.

Still, the story of Job is misleading if one interprets it literally, as the young man of *The Repetition* does, expecting a restoration of his original self. Only at the end of the book, when he learns that his former fiancée is engaged does he realize he cannot recapture himself on the same level on which he was before the intrusion of the transcendent. The true repetition is not a simple resumption of the self but an elevation onto a higher level of consciousness. After having gone through the infinite resignation, man can never be the same. To be forever resigned to one's unmarried state and, at the same time, to expect marriage is simply a contradiction. Job merely teaches that the eternal and the temporal are to be maintained simultaneously, but he does not teach *how* this is to be done. The time "redeemed" from eternity cannot be the same as man's original temporal order: eternity opens a new dimension in existence which makes a simple return to the past impossible. If the young man had understood this from the beginning, he would not have been concerned about the outcome of the temporal event.

> What is called reality would in a deeper sense be of no importance to him. He would have drained off religiously all the dreadful consequences contained in the occurrence. Though reality were to turn out differently it would not change him essentially.[17]

The repetition, then, is in fact not a repetition at all, but a transformation of the self to a higher level of existence, in which the ethical stage of freedom is sublated in the triple sense of annulled, preserved, and elevated.

It is precisely this transformation which makes the repetition into a religious rather than an ethical movement. Only the movement of faith accomplishes the paradoxical task of giving up the temporal and, at the same time, preserving it on a higher level. In the story of Job this movement is never mentioned—nothing indicates that Job *believed* in the restoration of his possessions. And yet, faith alone is able to redeem time from eternity. No one but the Knight of Faith believes in the real restoration of freedom. Job is religious only in a negative way: he knows that the transcendent is above all immanent categories and that the immanent may never be sacrificed to the transcendent, but he does not hope to have the immanent restored to its own right by the transcendent, as Abraham did when he was about to kill Isaac on Mount Moriah.

Faith alone solves the dialectical tension between the transcendent and the immanent, the eternal and the temporal. No autonomous ethical movement can reconquer the temporal once the eternal has interrupted its flow: "All God's doing . . . the ruins he makes, none can rebuild, his imprisonment none can escape. . . ."[18] The temporal can be restored only *from within the eternal* and this is precisely what faith does. Jean Wahl accurately describes the movement:

> The absolute had us, in the suspension of the ethical, violently separated from the real, had turned us against it; then it revealed itself in its infinite aspect, and first became a sanctuary in our flight from the real; this was the movement of infinite resignation; finally, in the movement of faith, it violently returns us to the real and allows us to reconquer and transform it. Man recaptures himself outside the temporal and restores the temporal to himself.[19]

Once man admits the eternal and resigns the temporal, he becomes unable to return to the temporal by an immanent ethical movement. The impulse now must come from the transcendent. Man's autonomous freedom can be restored only by the transcendent to which he has resigned it. Thus, in the religious attitude, the autonomy of freedom takes its origin from the theonomy of the transcendent, and the immanent movement of freedom ends in the paradox of faith. Resignation is the last autonomous movement of freedom; it would be its downfall and destruction, were it not followed by the transcendent movement of faith. Thus the very preservation of freedom's autonomy requires that it be completed by the theonomy of faith.

### The Intrinsic Limitation of Freedom: Guilt and Repentance

For a full understanding of this movement of faith, the failure of ethical striving must be considered from still another point of view: as guilt and sin. Thus far, the transcendent has merely been considered as an extrinsic limitation of freedom, an intrusion from without. But, as we saw already in *Either/Or* II, freedom also has its intrinsic limitations: it leads to its own downfall, and this is expressed in repentance.

*Fear and Trembling* describes this intrinsic limitation of freedom, and shows how the ethical order leads to its destruction by its own internal contradictions. For the sake of argument, Kierkegaard here adopts the view of his main adversary, Hegel, and defines the ethical as the individual will elevated to the universal level of reason. But whereas, for Hegel, individual freedom succeeds in realizing itself through the universal, for Kierkegaard this attempt results in failure and the individual is ultimately thrown back upon himself. All ethical striving ends in guilt and guilt places the individual outside the universal sphere of ethics. "An ethics which disregards sin is a perfectly idle science; but if it asserts sin, it is *eo ipso* well beyond itself."[20]

Repentance then is no longer a moment of the ethical consciousness, as it still was in *Either/Or*; it is its destruction, or, as Jean Wahl puts it, it completes the ethical by destroying it. "As soon as sin makes its appearance, ethics comes to grief precisely upon repentance, for repentance is the higher ethical expression, but precisely as such it is the deepest ethical self-contradiction."[21] Repentance, however, marks not merely the end of the ethical stage, but also the transition to the next stage. It is not only the nostalgic regret of the loss of the universal: in a negative way, it already attempts to return to the universal and to lead freedom back into autonomous self-realization. Yet, by repentance alone the individual cannot be restored *in statum pristinum*. "By his own strength he can make the movement of repentance, but for that he uses up absolutely all his strength, and hence he cannot by his own strength return and grasp reality."[22]

Precisely because it abandons the immanent and autonomous order of freedom without being able to return to it, repentance is equated with the movement of infinite resignation, the prelude to faith, described in *The Repetition* and in the first chapters of *Fear and Trembling*. In the story of Agnes and the Merman it is by repentance, rather than by trial (as it was in the cases of Abraham and Job) that the individual is taken out of the universal. Just as resignation, it breaks through the self-enclosed ethical sphere, and, like resignation, it is unable by itself to return to the order of freedom. In repentance the Merman makes the cloister-movement —he withdraws from the autonomous realization of the self—but he is unable to return to the world. "The man who has performed the cloister-movement has only one movement more to make, that is, the movement of the absurd."[23]

*Fear and Trembling* shows that the immanent choice of the self is by its own intrinsic necessity ultimately confronted with the transcendent. It refutes Hegel's position that freedom becomes absolute by realizing itself in the objective, the universal. For Kierkegaard freedom becomes fully authentic and therefore absolute only by separating itself from the universal with which it had identified itself in the ethical movement.[24] Even if the religious movement restores the universal—if the Merman were able to marry Agnes—this new universality is different from the one toward which the ethical strives, for it has been gained by virtue of the absurd, that is, by virtue of the exception. It is obvious, then, that the return to the autonomous sphere of freedom is not a simple repetition of the past, as the story of Job might still lead one to think. Once a man has become an exception to the ethical order by trial (as Job or Abraham) or by guilt (as the Merman and as every man who falls short of his ethical ideals), he will always remain an exception. The religious choice is a return to the self, but not a return to the past.

For Hegel, freedom becomes absolute by transcending its subjectivity in an objective universal order. Through this objectivation process the Spirit gradually integrates any form of transcendence with its own immanence, and the absolute consists precisely in this *integration* of the transcendent with the immanent. For Kierkegaard, on the contrary, freedom becomes absolute in the conscious *opposition* of the immanent to the transcendent. By the mediation process Hegel constantly returns the transcendent, which appears in the dialectical opposition, to the immanent. But for Kierkegaard a transcendence which can be mediated with the immanent is no longer transcendent. The finite spirit chooses its authentic, that is, its absolute, self only when it *opposes* its own immanence to an absolutely transcendent, which cannot be mediated. This irreducible opposition of the immanent and the transcendent reaches full expression when the autonomous ethical order is suspended by a transcendent religious order. Such a suspension of the immanent ethical order was God's command to Abraham to sacrifice his son, a command which conflicts with the universal natural law. More frequently, however, man comes into conflict with this universal order through his ethical failures. The religious breaks through the universal; from an ethical point of view, it is always an exception which cannot be morally justified. If Abraham had acted according to the universal, he would never have sacrificed Isaac and would have considered God's command to be a temptation. The religious attitude has no objective, universal expression. It is the return of subjective freedom to itself after its attempt to realize itself objectively. In faith man makes the leap into the realm of the impossible, after having renounced the possible in an act of infinite resignation. There is, then, no objective justification of faith, for faith means precisely that one has abandoned the objective order.

How far-reaching this distinction between the ethical and the religious order is, is illustrated in *Problem II* of *Fear and Trembling:* Is there such a thing as an absolute duty toward God? Kierkegaard here shows that the purely ethical notion of duty belongs to an immanent ethical order where there is no room for the transcendent as such. True, the ethical also has a religious implication: it suffices to refer to the religious orientation of the ethical attitude in *Either/Or* II. But as long as the religious is kept on the ethical level, the transcendent is caught in the universal and drawn into the immanent circle of human existence. Submerged in the ethical, the divine element is never "for itself."

> The whole existence of the human race is rounded off completely like a sphere, and the ethical is at once its limit and its content. God becomes an invisible vanishing point, a powerless thought, His power being only in the ethical, which is the content of existence.[25]

The real relation is the exact opposite: religion is not based on ethical duty, but duty receives its ultimate determination as duty from religion. "The individual determines his relation to the universal by his relation to the absolute, not his relation to the absolute by his relation to the universal."[26] In order to become a duty the ethical order must break through its own immanence and accept a new determination from the transcendent. But this religious determination subordinates the ethical to a higher sphere and thus reduces it to a relative position.[27]

### The Restoration of Freedom Through Faith

If faith is a stage in the development of freedom, it must obviously be more than the intellectual acceptance of a revealed truth; yet, in the *Philosophical Fragments* Kierkegaard defines faith entirely in terms of truth. What becomes of the existential attitude of Abraham in such a theory? To answer this question, we will have to consider Kierkegaard's concept of truth more closely.

In the *Philosophical Fragments* Kierkegaard opposes the philosophical concept of immanent truth to the Christian concept of a transcendent truth. In the former, the task of the teacher is to make himself superfluous and to help the pupil find the truth which exists in himself; in the latter, the teacher is not a mere occasion for the discovery of truth, but its cause. If truth is transcendent (philosophically this is a mere hypothesis), the pupil is not in the right position to understand it by himself, and the teacher must communicate to him not only the truth but also the condition for understanding it. But since an intellectual being is by his very nature made to understand the truth, there must be a reason why he is in a state of error (Kierkegaard presents no other alternative) with respect to this truth. Such a reason can only lie with the pupil, since man's Maker cannot contradict himself by creating a rational being who is unable to attain the truth. Johannes Climacus (Kierkegaard's pseudonym) therefore concludes that man's state of error is due to his own fault, a fault which Christianity calls sin. He further concludes that the pupil is unable to return to his initial state of truth after the teacher has made him aware of his error.

This whole argument is an obvious fallacy if one takes it to be a theory of objective truth. There is no reason why the pupil, once he has learned that he is in error, would not be able, of himself, to return to the truth. In fact, one would seem to imply the other.[28] But in dealing with the Christian hypothesis, Kierkegaard no longer uses the word truth in its logical sense, as the conformity of the mind's idea to an actual *Sachverhalt*, but in an ontological sense as being true to oneself. In the latter meaning of the word, it becomes understandable that once freedom has committed itself to the wrong choice (error), it is no longer at liberty to free itself and undo the choice. The first choice has constituted me what I am, even though what I am is not what I am supposed to be.

So, rather than intellectualizing religious categories, Kierkegaard in the *Philosophical Fragments* de-intellectualizes logical categories, confronting them with existence in its religious stage. Such a transformation of logical categories causes some serious difficulties. On the side of logic, the concept of truth becomes entirely devoid of its original meaning. On the religious side, the transcendent character of the "revealed truth" becomes intrinsically dependent upon the untruth of man. This position results in two equally untenable conclusions. Either one preserves the transcendence of God's revelation under any circumstances, and then sinfulness and existence (that is, being in time) are identical, which means that man becomes a sinner not by free choice, but by the very act of existing; or they are not identical, and then the revealed truth would not have been transcendent before the Fall, which means that the distinction between the immanent and the transcendent is reduced to the one between sinfulness and sanctity. Yet, these difficulties make it all the more obvious that the categories of logical truth are unfit to cope with Kierkegaard's notion of religious existence, and faith is to be seen as an existential act rather than as an acquisition of knowledge.

The non-cognitive character of the act of faith becomes even more apparent in Chapter III of the *Philosophical Fragments*, where the absolute paradox of Christianity is opposed not only to objective speculative thinking, but also to the paradox in the Socratic sense, the subjective passion of the mind exploring its own limits. Christianity here is no longer seen as a higher form of knowledge, but as a new form of existence.[29] Knowledge is either historical or eternal. In both cases the teacher is a mere occasion of learning. In the former case the historical existence of the teacher is important, but not essentially related to his doctrine; in the latter the unchanging doctrine of the teacher is important, whereas the historical events of his life become irrelevant. But in Christian faith man faces the paradox that the *Eternal* is made *historical*, and "no knowledge can have for its object the absurdity that the Eternal is the historical."[30] Knowledge is concerned with the doctrine or with the life of the man who held this doctrine. "But the disciple is in Faith so related to his teacher, as to be eternally concerned with his historical existence."[31] Kierkegaard therefore concludes that faith is not a form of knowledge.

Yet *Philosophical Fragments* teaches us more what faith is not, than what it is. To define faith as the absolute paradox is to describe merely what it looks like to the outsider, the philosopher. In the *Philosophical Fragments* Kierkegaard is primarily concerned to defend faith against the intrusion of philosophy rather than to understand its inner nature. In the *Concluding Unscientific Postscript,* on the contrary, he places faith in its proper context, existence. This also provides the ultimate reason why faith cannot be objective knowledge, since *existence*, that is, being in time, cannot be comprehended objectively. Objective knowledge can deal with being, but it never accounts for actual existence, that is, "anything which is, only because it *exists* or has existed and not simply because it is."[32] Not the notion of being but the notion of *contingent* being, of coming into being, is beyond the reach of philosophy. Philosophy never comes close to immediate existence, for as soon as it gets hold of the lived experience, the latter becomes reflective and ceases to be immediate. As Kierkegaard puts it:

How does the System (of Hegel's philosophy) begin with the immediate? That is to say, does it begin with it immediately? The answer to this question must be an unconditional negative. If the System is presumed to come after existence, by which a confusion with an existential system may be occasioned, then the System is of course *ex post facto* and so does not begin immediately with the immediacy with which existence began.[33]

Nor does reflection reach the immediacy of existence at the

end, for by its very nature reflection is infinite and never brings itself to a halt. The reflecting person can stop his reflection and return to the immediate experience, but this he does by a resolution of the will, not because reflection has reached its immanent end.

Kierkegaard does not imply that existence is an irrational form of being, but only that in *existence* being and thought never coincide. Existence clarifies itself in the dialectical opposition to thought, but it is never identical with thought, as the real is with the ideal in Hegel's absolute. By the same token, an existing subject remains forever separated from its objective expression. Subjective freedom creates objectivity but it never becomes objective itself. For a man to exist as a free subject is to constitute objectivity, to create history and to express himself objectively, yet never to identify himself with this objective expression. A subject is *per se* an inwardness unable to communicate directly with others. To look at it in an objective way is to misunderstand it and to transform it into something which it is not.

*Definitive Constitution of the Self:*
*Freedom as Pure Subjectivity in Christian Faith*

Yet there is a *truth* of existence; but this truth does not consist in objective knowledge, or in a static relation. It lies in man's subjectivity, and, since subjectivity is freedom, it is a task to be accomplished. The difficulty of this task is that it cannot be achieved by any objective performance, but merely by being concerned with subjectivity itself. It consists in inwardness rather than in outward achievements. Kierkegaard calls it passion. Of course, this interiorization process, as any process of consciousness, takes place in dialogue with an objective term. Yet, contrary to the act of knowledge, this objective term cannot be immediately appropriated. For only if the object is repellent can the subject move inward and concentrate on its own interiority. Kierkegaard therefore concludes that the object must be repellent to reason, or paradoxical. "The paradoxical character of the truth is its objective uncertainty; this uncertainty is an expression for the passionate inwardness, and this passion is precisely the truth."[34] The passion of the spirit reaches its culmination, and therefore its highest subjective truth, in faith, for the object of faith is so transcendent that it cannot be objectively appropriated. As a result, the objective problem of truth, whether the ideal term of the relation coincides with the real object, becomes meaningless in the case of faith, since man can never attain the reality of God. The only truth of faith consists in relating the subject to the religious object in such a manner that the *relation itself* is a true relation to that which is beyond the subject's reach. The truth-element here shifts entirely from the *quid* (the object) to the *quo* (the way of intending the transcendent object). Applying this to man's acceptance of Christianity, Kierkegaard writes:

> Hence we do not here raise the question of the truth of Christianity in the sense that when this has been determined, the subject is assumed ready and willing to accept it. No, the question is to the mode of the subject's acceptance. . . . The subjective acceptance is precisely the decisive factor; and an objective acceptance of Christianity is paganism or thoughtlessness.[35]

The paradoxical, repulsive character of the object of faith, then, turns out to be its most valuable asset for the attainment of subjective truth. Objective certainty draws the subject away from itself toward the object. No commitment, no return upon oneself is required for the understanding of an objective truth. If the self is a free subject which constitutes itself in passionate interiority, then all objective certainty must ultimately disappear and make room for the subjective certainty of freedom. Kierkegaard expresses this in his definition of the highest truth for an existing subject, "an objective uncertainty held fast in an appropriation process of the most passionate inwardness."[36] When the subject has no objective certainty, it increases the "tension of that infinite passion which constitutes inwardness."[37]

Christianity is the greatest possible paradox, and, consequently, leads to the greatest inwardness. In the *Philosophical Fragments* Kierkegaard showed how any relation of a being in time to an eternal truth is paradoxical, because to be related to an existing subject the eternal must be placed *in time*, and this implies a beginning, a coming into being, which conflicts with the very essence of the eternal.

But Christianity is more than the paradoxical relation of a being in time to the eternal. It teaches that the temporal, far from being related in a paradoxical way to the eternal, has become intrinsically opposed to the eternal. "The Socratic paradox consisted in the fact that the eternal truth was related to an existing individual, but now existence has stamped itself upon the existing individual a second time."[38] In its dogma of Original Sin, Christianity teaches that the temporal has become wholly temporal, that is, temporal in such a way that it excludes the eternal. At the same time, the dogma of the Incarnation brings the temporal and the eternal together in a union so intimate as to be offensive even from a Socratic point of view, which nevertheless relates the eternal to the temporal in a paradoxical way. In the person of Christ eternity is no longer *related* to time (thereby becoming paradoxical); the eternal itself has become temporal and God *exists* in time. This is the absolute paradox, the absurd. Neither speculation nor historical knowledge can make this idea more acceptable, for it "involves the contradiction that something which can become historical only in direct opposition to all human knowledge, has become historical."[39]

The notion of the absurd is a complex one and it is impossible to reduce it to one single element. It involves the transcendence of the Eternal to an existing being, sinfulness by which this Eternal becomes *opposed* to the temporal, the union of the Eternal and the historical in one person, and, finally, the relatedness of one subject to another subject. So far, we have not considered the last element, the inter-subjective relation expressed in the act of faith. Indeed, this point, which was not even mentioned in the *Philosophical Fragments*, is strongly emphasized in the *Postscript*. In the *Postscript*, Kierkegaard does not say, as in the *Fragments*: God is transcendent, therefore a human being can have no objective knowledge of him; instead he says: God is a subject and therefore exists only for subjectivity in inwardness.[40] Kierkegaard here implies that the truth of the relation to another subject is constituted in the very act in which I approach this subject. A subject cannot be grasped by an objective process of adequation to a pre-existing reality. In fact, a subject never pre-exists after the mode of an object: it is essentially openness, indetermination, freedom. And only in concentrating on my relation itself rather than on the pre-existent reality, can I do full justice to this openness. Any other approach to a subject, a person, degrades him to an object, a fixed and closed entity—and is therefore essentially *untrue*. This is not to deny that the *other* has an objective aspect as well, for, at least in the case of a human being, I perceive him *in* a world of objects; yet, beyond this objectivity, a true understanding of a subject must account for the openness, the self-determination of the other.

This is eminently true for man's relation to God because God alone is entirely free, so free that he transcends any objective expression. He cannot be captured in even the highest objective form, and any attempt to make him into an object of rational knowledge reduces him to a finite god, an idol. For that reason, Kierkegaard can say that whether I have a relation to the true God matters less than whether I have a true relation to God.

> If one who lives in the midst of Christianity goes up to the house of God, the house of the true God, with the true conception of God in his knowledge, and prays, but prays in a false spirit; and one who lives in an idolatrous community prays with the entire passion of the infinite, although his eyes rest upon the image of an idol: Where is there more truth? The one prays in truth to God though he worships the idol; the other prays falsely to the true God, and hence worships in fact an idol.[41]

That the truth of the relation to another subject is in the relation itself rather than in its conformity to the "object" is not only the case with respect to God. It is equally true for the relation to another human being. Unfortunately, Kierkegaard's religious individualism prevented him from developing this aspect of intersubjectivity which nevertheless seems to follow from his notion of subjective truth. To understand the other truly, I must accept him not as someone who *is*, but as someone who is *free;* and therefore essentially unfinished. As long as I *know* the other, in the sense that

I can predict how he will react, what he will say, and even how he will say it, I consider him something "finished" and I do not really understand him. Only in a subjective relationship (of faith or love), in which he breaks through all the objective categories that I had built around him, does the other reveal himself and does he become *true*. In the subjective relation to the other I permit him to become himself and to actualize the possibilities of his freedom. I understand him as a free being in the passion of a subjective relation; as long as I consider him an object, I regard him as already constituted and thereby overlook his most essential trait: to be free, self-constituting.

The complex dialectic of subjectivity unites the two opposite aspects of human freedom: that it is at once self-constituting and yet dependent. Self-choice and self-dependence are equally essential to freedom. For Kierkegaard the self is a relation to itself, and this implies that the self is essentially dynamic: to relate oneself actively to oneself means to choose oneself to be free.[42] Yet this relation to itself is also a relation to that which constitutes the relation. The human self is therefore essentially a derived relation, that is, a relation which "in relating itself to its own self relates itself to another."[43]

Kierkegaard is the first modern philosopher to place man's relation to God in the very heart of the self. Rather than construct a philosophy of religion, as his idealistic predecessors did, Kierkegaard laid the foundation for a religious philosophy by making freedom in the very act of self-constitution dependent upon the transcendent. At the same time he has avoided the perennial danger that threatens human autonomy in any philosophy which founds man's self-realization on a concept of creation (this is the objection made by Sartre and Merleau-Ponty against the *Weltanschauung* of the Christian—an objection which Duméry tries to answer in his *Philosophy of Religion*). Kierkegaard escapes this pitfall by making freedom into the very essence of the self. Even in its dependence the self (and the self alone) must constitute itself by freely choosing and accepting this dependence. For Kierkegaard a dependence which is not actively asserted does not enter into the constitution of the self as such. Only when the transcendent is freely accepted does it become a real transcendent. This is precisely the paradox for Kierkegaard's philosophy, that the transcendent in order to be transcendent must be brought into relation with an immanence which rejects that relation. Kierkegaard's *self* then, is not a homogeneous one; it is based on the most profound opposition between two mutually exclusive poles. The act of faith is precisely the attempt to integrate these two contradictory elements within oneself not by reconciling them (for they are irreconcilable) but by accepting the opposition itself as a manifestation of man's fundamental insufficiency, receiving thereby the entire immanence from the transcendent, in virtue of the absurd.

## NOTES

1. Some contemporary philosophers have followed his lead (Marcel, Buber, Jaspers), but none of them has posed the problem with the same sharpness and precision, nor has any of them equalled Kierkegaard's influence on modern thought.

2. Kierkegaard's *oeuvre* is not *merely* philosophical. In fact, he is primarily a theologian. This was my thesis in *Kierkegaard As Theologian* (New York: Sheed and Ward, 1963).

3. Søren Kierkegaard, *Either/Or*, trans. by David Swenson and Lillian Swenson (Princeton: Princeton University Press, 1944), II, 179.

4. *Ibid.*, p. 184.

5. *Ibid.*, p. 188.

6. *Ibid.*, p. 182.

7. That Kierkegaard here describes his own problem is obvious enough from a diary text which was used in the diapsalmata of *Either/Or*, Vol. I. "There is nothing more dangerous to me than remembering. The moment I have remembered some life relationship, that moment it ceased to exist. People say that separation tends to revive love. Quite true, but it revives it in a purely poetic manner. The life that is lived wholly in memory is the most perfect conceivable, the satisfactions of memory are richer than any reality, and have a security that no reality possesses. A remembered life-relation has already passed into eternity, and has no more temporal interest." *Ibid.*, pp. 31-32.

8. The English word "repetition" does not have all the connotations which *gjentagelse* has for Kierkegaard. In an unpublished commentary (which can now be found in *Søren Kierkegaard's Papirer*, ed. by P. A. Heiberg, V. Kuhr, and E. Torsting (Copenhagen, 1909-1948 IV B, 117), he interprets *at gjentage sig* as *at tage sig selv tilbage*, which Lowrie in the

Introduction to the English version of *The Repetition* translates as "to withdraw" but which I would rather translate as "to recapture oneself," or to "resume oneself." I would even suggest that *The Resumption* or *The Reassertion* might be a better title than *The Repetition*.

9. *Søren Kierkegaard's Papirer*, IV B 117, p. 47.

10. Kierkegaard, *The Repetition*, trans. by Walter Lowrie (Princeton: Princeton University Press, 1941), pp. 3-4.

11. We recognize an idea which was to be developed more fully by Bergson.

12. *Papirer*, IV B 177, p. 38.

13. It is obvious that the meaning of the word "transcendent" here is different from the previous paragraph in which it referred to an essential character of freedom (as opposed to thought). Here it refers to that which transcends freedom itself and in no way belongs to its autonomous movement.

14. *The Book of Job*, 11: 11-15 (*The Holy Bible*, trans. Ronald Knox, New York: Sheed and Ward, 1950).

15. *Job*, 27: 1-7 (Knox trans.).

16. *Kierkegaard's Papirer*, IV B 177, trans. Walter Lowrie's Introduction to *The Repetition*, p. xx.

17. *The Repetition*, p. 157.

18. *Job*, 12: 13-15.

19. Jean Wahl, *Etudes Kierkegaardiennes* (Paris: Aubier, 1959), p. 200.

20. Kierkegaard, *Fear and Trembling*, trans. Walter Lowrie (Princeton: Princeton University Press, 1941), p. 152.

21. *Loc. cit.*

22. *Ibid.*, pp. 153-154.

23. *Ibid.*, p. 150.

24. "L'absolu pour Hegel était ce qui unit absolument, il est pour Kierkegaard, du moins il est avant tout, ce qui sépare absolument" (Jean Wahl, *op. cit.*, p. 131).

25. *Fear and Trembling*, p. 102.

26. *ibid.*, p. 105.

27. *Loc. cit.*

28. The argument becomes even stranger in the third chapter. Kierkegaard shows how reason, in its passion to go to the limits of itself, hits upon the *unknown* which Johannes Climacus, without further ado, identifies with "God." He then argues that the *unknown* must be the absolutely different, that which is absolutely unlike man. "But if God and man are absolutely different, this cannot be accounted for on the basis of what man receives from God, for insofar they are akin. Their unlikeness must therefore be explained by what man receives from himself, or by what he has brought upon his own head. But what can this unlikeness be? Aye, what can it be but sin; since the unlikeness, the absolute unlikeness, is some-

thing that man has brought upon himself" (*Philosophical Fragments*, Princeton University Press, 1962), p. 58. It is true, indeed, that if man accepts the idea of God, then he must have some likeness to him, and an absolute unlikeness (supposing that it were possible) would be due to himself. But Kierkegaard fails to show that the *unknown* is the "absolutely different," and when the idea of the absolutely different does not fit with the rational notion of God, he reverts to the concept of sin rather than drop the identification itself.

29. Cf. K. Olsen Larsen, "Zur Frage des Paradoxbegriffes," in *Symposium Kierkegaardianum* (Copenhagen, 1955), pp. 130-147.

30. *Philosophical Fragments*, p. 76.

31. *Loc. cit.*

32. Kierkegaard, *Concluding Unscientific Postscript*, trans. David Swenson, Introduction by Walter Lowrie (Princeton, 1944), p. 99.

33. *Ibid.*, p. 101.

34. *Ibid.*, p. 183.

35. *Ibid.*, p. 116.

36. *Ibid.*, p. 182.

37. *Ibid.*, p. 182.

38. *Ibid.*, p. 189.

39. *Loc. cit.*

40. *Ibid.*, pp. 179-80.

41. *Ibid.*, pp. 178-79. The fact that Kierkegaard talks about the "true God" in one case, and an "idol" in the other, shows clearly that the matter is not entirely left to the individual subjectivity. There is indeed an objective datum, but it is not made objective by a self-sufficient process of knowledge: it is *given* by a transcendent revelation, and in that sense, it is not objective at all.

42. Kierkegaard, *Training in Christianity*, trans. by Walter Lowrie (New York, 1941), p. 159.

43. Kierkegaard, *The Sickness Unto Death*, trans. by Walter Lowrie (New York: Doubleday Anchor, 1958), p. 146.

# 3
# Hegel's Religion as Representation

With Hegel, philosophy of religion moves decisively beyond the subjectivity of the Kantian tradition. Once the process of consciousness comes to be viewed as an integral part of a spiritual process, the decisive question is no longer: What can we know? but: How (i.e., in which mode) do we know what we know? Philosophical emphasis shifts from the subjective act to the terminus of the act. However, Hegel's "turn to the object" by no means signifies a return to precritical thought. His philosophy of religion incorporates the entire Kantian problematic. Not only does his theory of representation rely heavily on Kant's treatment of the imagination, but the very need to view the transcendent terminus in symbolic representation bears Kant's mark. Still the differences are substantial. They appear not only in the particular mode in which philosophy treats the specific object of religion, but also in the entirely different relation between philosophy as a whole and its object. While Kant's philosophy "made room for faith" Hegel's embodies it.

## The Education of Consciousness

Hegel's theory of religion cannot be understood through his philosophy of religion alone. Since the finite finds its ultimate justification in the absolute which without the religious representation could not be thought, the entire science of philosophy, even in its most universal determinations, deals with a godly reality. Philosophy explains the content of religion when it explains itself. To be sure, the two do not entirely coincide and therefore a special branch of philosophy is needed to understand the specific, limited

53

truth of the religious intentionality. Yet the full truth of its content becomes manifest only in philosophy as a whole, not in the philosophical understanding of religion as such. This appears clearly in the final paragraphs of the *Encyclopedia*. The first of the so-called "syllogisms" of the Spirit basically coincides with the first syllogism of religion. Yet out of this religious starting point philosophy develops its own self-understanding independently of the religious representation: it is in this philosophical development rather than in its theological explication that religion attains its ultimate truth.

To attribute the fullness of religious truth to philosophy as a whole is not to take it away from religion proper. For philosophical truth is attained *in* and *through* the self-development of religion. Those preliminary stages of consciousness on its way to becoming Spirit which the *Phenomenology* describes, the unhappy consciousness, the ethical attitude, faith and its struggle with Enlightenment, the aesthetic world of the Greeks, mark only so many steps in the "itinerarium mentis ad spiritum" because they are also ascending stages of religious awareness.

The need to surpass each of these moments by no means entails that religion itself is a transitional state of mind. Certainly, in his student days Hegel had dreamed of overcoming the Christian religion of separation in some sort of romantic-Greek awareness of infinity in and through finite harmony. But well before writing the *Phenomenology* he had abandoned this mirage of the past for a more tragic vision. Ours is a broken world in which the infinite has become severed from its infinite ideal. They can be reunited only through a full awareness of their separation, such as the Christian religion achieves in its doctrines of Fall and Redemption. The essential principle of Christianity holds true for all genuine religion. "L'âme religieuse est une âme divisée."[1] Yet by converting the entire sensible existence into a symbol, a receptacle of the infinite, religion reintegrates the divided consciousness and conveys to the finite mind "a sense of its own unity with the unchangeable."[2] In Christian doctrine Hegel saw the education of the Western mind to philosophical truth.

Again and again the *Phenomenology* returns to the theme of separation and reunion so essential to the spiritual education of consciousness. The collapse of the ancient culture in the self-conscious nihilism of the classical comedy marks the most poignant instance of the mind's tragic division.

> It is the consciousness of the loss of everything of significance in this certainty of itself, and of the loss even of this certainty of self—the loss of substance as well as of self: it is the bitter pain . . . God is dead.[3]

Christianity both symbolizes this pain and deepens it in the physical death of the God-man on the cross. In the doctrine of Original Sin separation and self-estrangement are declared to be the very essence of man. Yet in the God-man dies the "wickedness" of the finite which has willfully isolated itself in asserting an independent finitude.

In the *Phenomenology* Hegel attempted to resolve the crisis of modern consciousness which he regarded as profoundly religious. Yet the *Phenomenology* is not a book *about* religion as such, however extensively it deals with it. Even the discussion of revealed faith in the seventh chapter does not treat religion for its own sake, but only insofar as it *educates* the mind to become aware of its own infinity.

## The Religious Imagination

The discussion of religion in the *Encyclopedia* and its elaboration in the *Lectures on the Philosophy of Religion* is of a different nature. Here Hegel attempts to understand religion in its own right. That religion left to itself fails to reach full self-understanding does not make it "subordinate" to a "higher" form of consciousness. On the contrary, the discussion of the *Encyclopedia* rather suggests that philosophy is subordinate to religion. In defining religion as *representation* Hegel assigns it a position intermediate between such subjective forms of consciousness as feeling, faith and certainty which we encountered in the earlier part of the *Phenomenology*, and, on the other side, thought.[4] The reason why the religious representation is able to mediate thought is that its own internal dynamism turns it into thought itself. Religion therefore may be said to be *both* representation *and* thought.[5]

Hegel's theory of representation incorporates three major insights of his predecessors about the role of the imagination: its de-temporalizing function (Kant), its creative force (Fichte), its religious impact (Schelling). For Kant the imagination construes representations without subjecting them to critical analysis. It synthesizes appearances; it is not concerned with the conditions which insert this synthesis into an objective world. A representation develops into a full-fledged image when the imaginative function lingers over it rather than delivering it outright to the objectifying process of the understanding. If this occurs, the representation becomes detached from the stream of sensation and synthesized into an independent unit which resists being absorbed by the continuous totality of the *real world*. It is precisely this self-sufficient independence which predestines the image for aesthetic expression. Kant describes the activity of the imagination as a synthesis *in accordance with time*. Of course, temporality is not restricted to the productive imagination, since succession is the very form of sense perception. Yet it is only by means of new temporal syntheses that percepts can be detached from the continuous stream of perception and made into independent representations. Only by withdrawing from the stream of succession does the representation acquire its characteristic inwardness. This withdrawal does not sever all relationship to ordinary time but places the representation in an independent position with respect to this succession. The first and simplest form in which it may achieve this is by "taking refuge in the past."[6] Hegel develops this de-temporalization through the past in his theory of recollection.

The creative power of the imagination is commonly associated with Fichte's name, but it was already introduced by Kant. To reproduce a percept, as the imagination does, is to take it out of its original mode of givenness and to place it in a temporal setting which essentially transforms it. What results is not merely a reproduction, but as Kant knew, a novel production. Liberated from the actuality of perception the future is no longer tied to the past in rectilinear determination. By escaping from the *merely* present the imagination makes the future into a genuine possibility. This explains why the mind's awareness of freedom grows with the trust in its powers of imagination. Kant's theory of the *productive* synthesis inspired Fichte (and to some extent also Schelling) to conceive the imagination as the moving power of the mind. For Fichte the productive imagination precedes all conscious activity and thus allows the mind to be totally autonomous, that is, at once determining (through the imagination) and determined (as actual consciousness).[7] The imagination alone provides all the determinations of the real, even the complex articulations of the object-appearance which Kant ascribed to the categories of the understanding.[8] Nor is there any fundamental distinction, as Kant assumed, between the sensuous intuition and the non-intuitive understanding, for the phenomenal intuition is the first stage of a process which eventually will be liberated from its spatio-temporal setting and converted into a reflective cognition, valid for all time, that substitutes for the direct apprehension of the object the permanent symbol of a concept. The productive imagination is spontaneous yet not random, for it constitutes the very laws which structure the real. Thus it produces the controlled concepts of the scientist and the philosopher as well as the phantasies of the artist and the myths of the primitive. Nor is its productivity limited to the cognitive order. The very ideals of freedom by which the mind attempts to overcome its finite determinations are as much constituted by the productive imagination as the determinations themselves.

Schelling developed Fichte's insight in showing how the myth, and therefore the religious conceptualization, is rooted in the productive imagination. Indeed, for him the imagination is essentially religious. The perfect unity of the real and the ideal in God, which became lost in the finitude of nature, is reconstituted by the creative imagination, the *Einbildungskraft*, that is, the power of "uniformation." The imagination reunites what is one in God. Its divine character becomes manifest in its exclusive power to create the representations of the divine—the gods.[9] In the gods the imagination combines the reality of nature with the ideality of spirit. Hegel will follow Schelling's insight. Yet Schelling failed to distinguish adequately the mythic-religious representation from the aesthetic image. For him the prime object of art is mythology. Hegel will be more cautious in his interpretation of the relation between the aesthetic and the mythic-religious imagination. Let us now consider his own theory of religious representation.

Hegel discusses it in the section on psychology, the final moment of the subjective spirit in the *Encyclopädie*. Once the mind has overcome the opposition between itself and the object-out-there in the early stages of consciousness, it gradually synthesizes the two essential functions of knowledge: one by which it makes the object of consciousness its own *(das Seinige)* and the other by which it projects it into an ontic reality and thereby allows it to transcend a purely mental existence *(das Seiende)*. In the representation the mind becomes aware that its content is not bound by the space and time restrictions of the sensuous intuition. What I intuit in space and time is *eo ipso* singularized to a *here* and *now*. The representation preserves the intuitive content, yet *re*-presents it in a way which is no longer tied to the *here* and *now*. The content is still represented temporally—rather than in the universal form of thought—but the temporality of the representation is no longer that of the sense intuition: it is, so to speak, a free temporality of the subject.

The intuitive content becomes part of the mind's *own* world, that is, the world which it "owns," by being converted from a mere vision of the world into a symbol of the mind's spiritual life. The impact of time on the inner life appears clearly in the first form of representation, the *recollection (Erinnerung)*. Etymologically the term recollection denotes both a recalling of the past and an internalizing of a present awareness.

> Intelligence, as it at first recollects the intuition, places the content of feeling in its own inwardness—in a space and a time of its own. In this way that content is an *image* or picture, liberated from its original immediacy and abstract singleness amongst other things, and received into the universality of the ego. The image loses the full complement of features proper to intuition, and is arbitrary or contingent, isolated, we may say, from the external place, time, and immediate context in which the intuition stood.[10]

By being de-temporalized the recollected representation becomes detached from its original setting. This enables it to stand for a number of similar experiences and to achieve a certain measure of universality. Yet this representation does not attain the logical coherence of thought. Its coherence remains one of succession and juxtaposition.

> The coherence of the determinations appears to the representation as successive, not necessary (as only in the notion). The necessary interconnection of the determinations of the absolute content can be grasped only by the timeless, non-sensible notion. The representation retains these determinations as a succession in time. In religion we narrate. The abstract content comes first, its concrete fulfillment appears as a natural event, that is, as a happening in time.[11]

In the recollection the singular intuition is assumed into a representation with a universal content.[12] The form remains singular. Yet by omitting a number of particularities the recollection attains a meaning-potential which far surpasses that of any single intuition. The universality of the representation, then, consists in the transcendence of the content with respect to the singular form.

## Image and Symbol

The interiorization of the *Vorstellung* with respect to the intuition appears even clearer in the productive imagination or *phantasy* which totally abandons the order of succession of the original intuitions in favor of a succession in the subject's inner life. The images of phantasy are no longer experienced as *re*produced, but rather as produced by the mind. At the same time they bring the mind closer to the awareness of an ontic, that is, a not-purely mental reality. The process of interiorization is also one of objectification. While the mind progressively interiorizes its images it simultaneously rids itself of the subjectivism of the senses by opening up a new sort of exteriority *within* the interiority of the mind.[13] In the phantasy image the mind associates a number of intuition images moulding them into one universalized totality. The process of association is directed by an overriding representation which itself is not an image. The guiding representation may play an even more universalizing role by endowing images with a symbolizing power which allows them to transcend their concrete determinations. Thus we obtain concrete universal representations which Hegel calls *symbols,* and abstract ones, called *signs* and *allegories.* Strangely enough, Hegel rates signs higher than symbols. For him the symbol retains too much of its original image autonomy to be entirely clear in its meaning.[14] The sign enjoys no such autonomy. To posit a sign is to refer directly to the signified, since the sign has no other meaning. "The sign differs from the symbol, an intuition whose own determination according to essence and notion is more or less the content which it expresses as symbol. In the sign, on the contrary, the content of the intuition and the content of what is signified remain unrelated."[15] What matters in the sign is that there is an intuitive form; *which one* is unimportant. "The sign retains nothing of itself; it sacrifices itself to its sense."[16]

The representations of symbols, allegories and poetic images prepare the objectivity of thought by raising the question of their own objectivity status. In *representing* something I am critically aware that a question about its objective reality may be raised, even though I choose not to raise it. This indicates that the representation already points beyond the merely accepted intuition toward the object *in itself.*[17] The representation knows itself to be only a representation. One commentator describes Hegel's representational consciousness as "picture thinking in which the pictures are recognized as such."[18] But to know a representation to be *only* a representation is to relate it to objective, not purely representational being and thus to initiate the problem of objectivity. *What* constitutes objectivity is not revealed in the representation which remains too much caught in subjectivity to distinguish the real from the non-real. It merely posits its content as objectively *problematic.* To do more would require that the mind be conscious of its own power to constitute the real as real. The representational consciousness merely raises a question and invites a deeper reflection which will eventually result in full objectivity. To *know* will consist in realizing that the representation represents *something.* The representation *re*-presents objective reality by letting a particular intuition take its place. Thought will *present* reality itself and thereby reveal the full meaning of the representation.

In his *Lectures on the Philosophy of Religion* Hegel strongly emphasizes the objective character of the representation. It is precisely the representation which prevents the subjectivity of religious feeling to degenerate into self-deification, fanaticism and intolerance.[19] The religious representation first states the truth which philosophy will present in the form of thought. "Religion is the true content but in the form of representation. The substantial truth is not given first by philosophy."[20] The religious mind does not grasp its determinations in their intrinsic connectedness. It presents them in succession and juxtaposition, while thought shows the determinations in their development and, consequently, in their overarching unity. Thus in speaking of God religious man will mention a number of unrelated attributes: God is just, but he is *also* merciful. The representation strings together determinations which it is unable to *think* simultaneously.

Representations are not identical with "images." This is particularly important for understanding Hegel's philosophy of religion. In religion images are never used for their own sake, but always as *symbols* and *allegories* of a transcendent content. Moreover, the religious representation includes also mythical or historical developments.[21] The true content of religion can be *represented* by myth or historical narrative but it cannot be adequately expressed by them. A mere report of events can never convey the transcendent content of a religious faith. Finally, the religious representation includes even non-sensuous and, by all appearances, purely spiritual concepts. Creation is such a concept.

> When we say: the world has been created, we refer to an activity which substantially differs from any empirical one. Even the expression "activity from which the world proceeded," although abstract is still representational and notional, insofar as the two sides are not connected in the form of necessity: the connection which in itself is entirely unique and incomprehensible is expressed and signified in an analogy with natural life and events.[22]

The image is always present in the religious representation, but usually in a subordinate function. The transcendent content overburdens it to the point where it loses its original meaning. This transcendent character makes the religious representation basically iconoclastic with respect to images.

Religion has a polemical aspect insofar as its content cannot be perceived immediately in the sensuous intuition or in the image, but only mediately by abstraction, this is, by elevating the imaginary and the sensible to a universal level. This elevation implies a rejection of the image. At first only the form would seem to be rejected, but in fact the content itself is affected insofar as the religious meaning is connected with the image and the image, the beautiful, precisely implies that the universal, the thought, the notion cannot be separated from the image. . . .[23]

Nevertheless, the religious representation always requires images, and the use of images is what distinguishes one religious faith from another. Thus Hegel describes Hinduism as a religion of fantasy, because the powers of the Hindu imagination are not subordinated to a higher instance: coherent images are all that is required for this sort of religious reality. The only criterion of the Hindu mythology is man's capacity to imagine it.[24] It is superfluous to point out the confident ignorance displayed in this simplistic interpretation of Hindu faith. The valuable point is that religious representation does not simply coincide with religious fantasy.

In Greek mythology the image is equally important, but it is controlled by an awareness of the divine as subjective and *free*. This freedom is still hidden in the many "powers" of nature. Nevertheless, in their aesthetic representation the powers reveal a subjective spontaneity which both surpasses and unites nature as the human spirit directs and animates the human body.[25] The aesthetic mythology of the Greeks conveys a religious transcendence insofar as the images of the gods are conceived as much more beautiful than man's image of himself. Indeed, the Greek gods may be said to represent man's ideal of himself. Precisely because of its idealized form was Greek mythology able to accommodate so harmoniously the ideal content of religion.[26] Religion consists in lifting the natural and moral powers which rule human life above their ordinary context. Rather than being a negation of the human, Greek mythology was nothing more than idealized humanity. The cult beautified life rather than changing it.

> In other forms of religion, sacrifice means to give up, to bring forward, to deprive oneself. But here . . . sacrifice consists in drinking the wine and eating the meat. . . . Thus higher meaning and enjoyment is given to all activities of life. Here one finds no self-denial, no apology for eating and drinking. But every occupation and pleasure of daily existence is made into a sacrifice.[27]

Yet the limitation of this ideal is that it is caught in its own aesthetic *image* character. The Greek gods, at least as we know them through Homer and Hesiod, became exclusively ideals of beauty. The more aesthetically perfect they grew, the more they lost their meaning as religious symbols, that is, as finite appearances which reveal an infinite *transcendence*. Their perfect containment within finite forms made them aesthetic before poets and sculptors made them into works of art. It was their own aesthetic potential which killed the Greek gods: their very conception demanded an artistic treatment which they could not religiously survive.

The problems inherent in Greek religion raise the more substantial question how the representation can *ever* become a symbol of transcendence. What could possibly allow an interiorized intuition to move beyond the purely immanent? To be sure, every representation, being by its very nature symbolic of the mind, transcends the purely sensible. Yet the specific transcendence of the religious act requires that the finite mind (symbolized in *any* representation) be itself transcended. How can a mere representation achieve this transcendence?

At this point Hegel's discussion of language takes on a crucial importance. Without words the representations are never able to convey a meaning that entirely surpasses its worldly origin. In a perceptive essay on the subject professor Vander Kerken has spelled out what Hegel merely implied: "The verbalization is constitutive of the religious representation: without it the representation would never move beyond a very primitive potentiality."[28] Language alone enables the representation to convey total transcendence by loosening the ties between the symbolized content and the symbolizing intuition. The verbalized representation replaces, in fact, the original, polymorphous intuition by one over which the mind exercises much greater control. Over and above the represented structure language imposes *its own* system of meaning, thereby reshaping it into a more articulate bearer of a spiritual content and endowing it with a wholly new kind of symbolism. But to convey a religious meaning language must, in addition, transcend its natural symbolism and be able to signify beyond its ordinary capacity. Thus to assert that God has begotten a son is to signify symbolically a relation which cannot be signified directly. The "wrath of God" is clearly a metaphor and so are the tree of knowledge, Pandora's box and Prometheus' education of the human race. Hegel tells us little about the distinctive character of this religious symbolism of language—how it differs from poetry. All we learn is that such language relates negatively to its pictorial representations without, however, liberating itself from them.[29] Yet Hegel brings out one characteristic: in the religious representation the various determinations "succeed" one another.[30] Thus religious language transforms its representations "into a series of events," historicizing a reality which, though dynamic, is not successive at all. In this narrative quality the religious representation displays its inherently *temporal* character. Even theology, its most speculative expression, still represents the relation between God and the world as a story. First, God exists without the world, *then* his creative act gives birth to the world. First, Divine Providence draws up a plan of salvation, *then* follows its historical execution.[31]

## Representation and Idea

How the speculative idea of God differs from the religious representation, becomes evident in a comparison between the three syllogisms of revealed religion[32] and the three speculative syllogisms that conclude the *Encyclopedia*.[33] The first syllogisms of both series describe God's inner life and are basically identical. Yet in the second religious syllogism the inner life of the Trinity is "succeeded" by an outward creation which enables the infinite Spirit to mediate itself with itself through the otherness of the finite. In the third syllogism this otherness is reintegrated with the infinite Spirit. In its ideal truth the infinite Spirit allows no such "separation into parts with a temporal and external sequence."[34] The moments of its self-articulation exist simultaneously and presuppose one another. In religious language, creation and redemption take place *within* God's intra-trinitarian life and the revelation rather than being an *opus-ad-extra* is essentially God's self-revelation.

The speculative syllogisms, then, do not follow in succession but presuppose one another as segments of a circle. The first syllogism articulates the inner life of the Absolute from its universal origin via its inner mediation to the concreteness of the Spirit. The religious terms of Father, Son and Holy Spirit have been replaced by the philosophical terms Logic, Nature, Spirit.

Nature, standing between the Spirit and its essence, sunders itself, not indeed to extremes of finite abstraction, nor itself to something away from them and independent—which, as other than they, only serves as a link between them: for the syllogism is *in the Idea* and Nature is essentially defined as a transition-point and negative factor, and as implicitly the Idea.[35]

The entire process of mediation displays an intrinsic necessity which it never attained in the purely descriptive religious presentation and which requires that the middle term (Nature) be justified through self-explication, not through the introduction of external elements. The same holds true for the justification of the new, justifying middle term (Spirit).

The religious syllogisms follow a different, extrinsic process in their succession of creation and redemption. Here God's self-mediation is presented exclusively as it *appears*, that is, as a manifestation which still needs to be mediated with the divine self-identity. Creation and redemption become *true* only once we understand that the *Erscheinung* (#574) is ultimately an appearance *of* the Absolute *for itself* rather than *for us*, and that its "otherness" is an internal one.

The second syllogism describes the movement whereby the Spirit returns the determination into the logical, universal principle and thereby makes it into the Idea's own determination. Without this interiorization otherness would be excluded from the Idea. Without the internalization of the Spirit God's self-manifestation would be wholly profane. In the trinitarian language of the first religious syllogism this means: "There is a creative work in which the Father externalizing Himself forgets Himself in order to let the Son be, *and* a work of restitution and divinization by the Spirit which results in the Idea and returns the Son to the Father."[36] Thus Nature, so opaque and self-sufficient in appearance, is perceived by reason as possessing neither self-subsistence nor permanence. Or as Hegel writes descriptively in the *Philosophy of Religion*: "The otherness is an immediate passing moment, the flash of lightning which instantly vanishes, the sound of a word the external existence of which disappears as soon as it is spoken and apprehended."[37] Earlier in discussing the notion of religion Hegel had already asserted that the external order of creation merely shadows the development of God's inner life.

> These two subjects *(Stoffe)*, God's internal development and the development of the universe, are not so absolutely different. God is the truth, the substance of the universe, not merely an abstract Other. They therefore may be considered to be the same subject; it is the intellectual, divine world, the divine life in Himself which develops. But this act of his life coincides with the life of the world in such a manner, however, that while the latter is mere appearance, the former is eternal. Hence the life of the world becomes manifest there in its eternal mode—*sub specie aeterni*. The finite world, nature, finite consciousness is the opposite, the other of the Idea. In God, as religion represents it, the other is his Son, that is, the other who in love remains within the Deity, and the Son is the truth of the finite world.[38]

Hegel elaborates this in his theory of the Word and the Kingdom of the Son in the fourth volume of the *Vorlesungen*. But, more importantly, the entire *Logic* develops the theory of divine manifestation. Hegel himself refers to the *Logic* as the primeval Word of the Absolute Idea, the Word which though it is external, immediately abolishes its own externality. But first we must consider the third syllogism which concludes the *Philosophy of Spirit*.

This syllogism completes what the second initiated, namely the mediation of the Spirit. For this mediation itself is based upon a particular relation between the Spirit and Nature. A particular difficulty in understanding this syllogism arises from the middle term which is described as "self-knowing reason." Does reason not become Spirit when it becomes self-knowing? But, if it does, Spirit is both the subject and the middle term of this syllogism. Indeed, thought does not become fully rational until the Spirit mediates *itself*. The particularity of Nature could not have been restored to the universality of the Logical Principle (in the second syllogism) without the mediating Spirit making itself conform to the particularity of Nature. In theological language, the Spirit is constituted as Divine Person only as Spirit *of the Son*. The universal Principle overcomes the finitude of the particular and the individual principles only insofar as it is *intrinsically related* to them (theology would say: as it is constituted as a person) and this requires the presence of the Spirit (the individual) *within* the Logical Principle (the universal). Therefore, in the ultimate movement of reason the Spirit must be its own mediator.

## The Logic as God's Self-Manifestation

On the basis of the syllogisms of the Spirit we must conclude that the *Logic* holds the last key to Hegel's religious thought. Once we establish the Absolute to be self-revealing, the logic of *manifestation as such* prior to any actual words, becomes the primary articulation of the Absolute. Hegel referred to his *Logic* as the theory of God before the creation of the world. The significance of the *Logic* cannot be fully appreciated until its universal metaphysical determinations are understood as the most fundamental self-expression of the Absolute. To be sure, the logical Idea does not reveal the concrete richness of the Absolute, as art, religion and their philosophical understanding do. The *Logic* expresses God's reality as it has become manifest not in nature, history, art or cult, but in pure thought. Yet since the nature of the Absolute is *spiritual*, the science of pure thought expresses that reality most completely.

This appears from the very beginning of the process of thinking, in the so-called Logic of Being. Hegel's discussion of the relation between the finite and the infinite starts from the divine infinite reality itself, rather than from our finite knowledge of it.

> Dualism, in putting an insuperable opposition between finite and infinite, fails to note the simple circumstance that the infinite is thereby only one of two, and is reduced to a particular, to which the finite forms the other particular. Such an infinite, which is only a particular, is co-terminous with the finite which makes for it a limit and a barrier: it is not what it ought to be, that is, the infinite, but is only finite. In such circumstances, where the finite is on this side, and the infinite on that,—this world as the finite, and the other world as the infinite,—an equal dignity of permanence and independence is ascribed to finite and to infinite.[39]

The theological significance of the *Logic* appears most clearly in the theory of essence. The reason is that the religious representation—and all of theology remains on the level of representation—occurs entirely within the essential reflection. Here we encounter those determinations which are commonly given as fundamental attributes of God: the ground of being (#121), the force (#136), the necessity (#147), the substance (#151), the cause. In the *Lectures on the Philosophy of Religion* (Bk II) Hegel has shown their theological necessity. But unless one studies their *essential* necessity in the *Logic*, such a theology must itself remain unfounded and the attributes mere applications from a different realm of necessity. The ultimate truth of religion, then, must come from philosophy and philosophy explains itself when it grounds religion.

The theory of essence becomes *true* only when the essential determinations are viewed in their relatedness, that is, in the *notion*. Since the religious representation never fundamentally *relates* its concepts to one another, the section on the notion is less *recog-*

*nizably* religious. Yet Hegel himself leaves no doubt about its religious import. In his Lectures on Absolute Religion he introduces the discussion of the Kingdom of the Son with the following statement: "We know from the notion the moment of differentiation and, more specifically, of the determinate differentiation."[40] It is from this self-differentiating notion that the rational necessity of a divine manifestation is derived. Moreover, in a *Zusatz* to the paragraph 161 of the *Logic* which describes the notion as *self-developing*, Hegel refers to the generation of the Son in the Trinity.

Of crucial importance here is the notion's negative reflection into itself whereby it posits itself as *different* but as different *through its own determination*. The very act in which the universal conceives itself as self-identical is also the one in which it posits itself as other. Yet the absolute negativity of this reflection entails a phenomenal division as well as a rational one. In the *Ur-theilung*, the ontological basis of the theory of judgment (Urteil = judgment), the notion undergoes a radical split by which it opposes itself to itself. The *Ur-theilung* allows the finite to exist distinct from the infinite. The separation of judgment constitutes the most fundamental articulation of that independence which nature did not possess in the eternal Logos. Being the self-reflection of the notion, judgment at first is no more than "the genuine particularity of the notion." Yet in the judgment this moment of particularity becomes disconnected from the universal, as the subject from the predicate, and "genuine" otherness originates. Thus judgment comes to express separation and finitude.

> Things from its point of view are said to be finite, because they are a judgment, because their definite being and their universal nature . . . though united indeed . . . are still elements in the constitution which are already different and also in any case separable.[41]

The logic of judgment must not be equated with the theology of creation, as Roger Garaudy has rightly insisted. Nevertheless, it is in the judgment that we find the most universal manifestation, the pure structure, of that alienation which the creation concretely realizes.[42]

However, the truth of judgment lies in the syllogism which re-unites the separate moments of the notion. Here the notion mediates between the singularity of the subject and the universality of the predicate in order to restore the identity which judgment had rent apart. In the syllogism the finite comes to be seen as an *integral part* of the infinite rather than as a reality *juxtaposed* to the infinite. To think the relation is to perceive the negation of the finite as "a negation of the Idea but a negation within the Idea and accomplished by the Idea."[43] In the Idea all otherness is internal otherness, all negation self-negation. But this also constitutes the limitation of the Idea. For the otherness of nature cannot be grasped through purely logical determination. In relating exclusively to itself and in being able to refer to anything beyond itself, the Idea adopts, in fact, the same immediate character as nature. What we have here is, on the one hand, the identity of all reality in its absolute origin, expressed in the self-identity of the Idea, and, on the other hand, the genuine otherness of contingent reality with respect to that origin, expressed in the non-ideality of nature. Thought and reality must remain opposed in an apparently invincible ignorance of each other's identity.

The Christian faith shows an exit out of this impasse in representing otherness first *within the identity* of the Trinity as the uncreated Word, and then *outside* this identity as creation. Above all, faith shows how the Spirit connects the two by assuming the entire creation into the divine identity of the Word. This supreme principle of faith is also the key principle of Hegel's philosophy. In the Preface to the *Phenomenology* Hegel had written that modern philosophy owed its deepest insight to the Christian faith, namely, that the Absolute is Spirit. This appears nowhere more clearly than in the outcome of the *Logic*. Without the concept of Spirit the *Logic* would never be able to cross the bridge from thought to reality. Philosophy would remain self-enclosed thought, unable to leave its own identity. The Spirit allows it to move beyond and to integrate the total otherness of nature with its self-identity.

It falls beyond the scope of this investigation to pursue the religious qualities of Hegel's concept of Spirit. My only concern here was to show how the content of religion provides not only the original impulse to Hegel's philosophy which then, as in the *Logic*, moves beyond the religious representation, but also how, at critical stages in its development, only a return to that representation permits philosophy to achieve its own ends.

## NOTES

1. Jean Wahl, *Le malheur de la conscience dans la Phénoménologie de Hegel* (Paris (1929), 1951), p. 19.

2. *Phänomenologie des Geistes* (Hamburg: Philosophische Bibliothek, 1952), p. 167. *The Phenomenology of Mind*, trans. J. B. Baillie (New York: Harper and Row, 1967), p. 261.

3. *Phënomenologie*, p. 523. *Phenomenology*, p. 752.

4. *Vorlesungen über die Philosophie der Religion* (Hamburg: Philosophische Bibliothek, 1925), I, p. 68.

5. Claude Bruaire, *Logique et religion chrétienne* (Paris, 1965), p. 42.

6. Mikel Dufrenne, *Phénoménologie de l'expérience esthétique* (Paris, 1953), p. 434.

7. *Grundlage der gesammten Wissenschaftslehre*, in *Sammtliche Werke*, Vol. I, ed. by J. H. Fichte (Berlin, 1845), p. 227.

8. *Grundriss des Eigentümlichen der Wissenschaftslehre*, in *Sammtliche Werke*, Vol. I, pp. 376-87.

9. *Sämtliche Werke*, ed. by Manfred Schröter (München, 1958), p. 410.

10. *Encyclopädie* (1831), p. 452; trans. William Wallace (Oxford: Clarendon Press, 1971).

11. *Vorlesungen über die Philosophie der Religion*, ed. Georg Lasson (Hamburg, 1966), Vol. I, p. 297.

12. *Encyclopädie*, #454.

13. André Léonard, *La foi chez Hegel* (Paris: Desclée, 1970), pp. 234-235.

14. This explains why the "symbolic" art of Egypt and the Orient ranks lowest in the *Lectures on Aesthetics*.

15. *Encyclopädie* #458 Zusatz.

16. Malcolm Clark, *Logic and System: A Study of the Transition from Vorstellung to Thought in the Philosophy of Hegel* (The Hague: Martinus Nijhoff, 1971), p. 63.

17. See, J. Hessing and J. G. Wattjes, *Bewustzÿn en Werkelijkheid*, Amsterdam, s.d., p. 339.

18. Clark, *Op. cit.*, p. 59.

19. *Vorlesungen über die Philosophie der Religion*, I, p. 286.

20. *Vorlesungen*, I, p. 299.
21. In *Vorlesungen*, I, p. 284, Hegel includes the myth in the image.
22. *Vorlesungen*, I, p. 113.
23. *Vorlesungen*, I, p. 285.
24. *Vorlesungen*, II, p. 144.
25. *Vorlesungen*, III, pp. 119-25.
26. *Vorlesungen*, III, p. 144.
27. *Vorlesungen*, III, p. 170.
28. Libert Vander Kerken, "De religieuze beleving als voorstelling" in *Tÿdschrift voor Philosophie* 34 (1972), p. 14.
29. *Vorlesungen*, I, 115. I have attempted to develop this point in *The Other Dimension* (New York: Doubleday, 1972), ch. 5.
30. *Encyclopädie* (1831) #565.
31. *Vorlesungen*, I, pp. 113-14.
32. *Encyclopädie* #567-570.
33. *Encyclopädie* #575-577.
34. *Encyclopädie* #571.
35. *Encyclopädie* (1831) #575. I have followed the translation of William Wallace: *Hegel's Philosophy of Mind* (Oxford University Press, 1971) except for the term *Geist* which I prefer to translate as *Spirit* rather than as *Mind*.
36. Claude Bruaire, *Logique et religion chrétienne*, p. 101.
37. *Vorlesungen*, IV, pp. 86-87.
38. *Vorlesungen*, I, p. 186. This text is taken from Hegel's own script, not from the notes of his students.
39. *Encyclopädie* (1831) #95 Zusatz, trans. William Wallace, pp. 176-77.
40. *Vorlesungen*, IV, p. 85b.
41. *Encyclopädie* (1831) #168, trans. William Wallace, p. 300.
42. Roger Garaudy, *Dieu est mort*, pp. 357-58. Cf. André Chapelle, *Hegel et la religion* II (Paris: Editions Universitaires, 1967), pp. 130-32.
43. G. Noel, *La Logique de Hegel*, p. 126.

# Part II
# The Search for a Method

# 4
# Husserl's Intentions of Experience

Even if Husserl had done nothing more than distinguish by his concept of intentionality what the religious act intends from the subjective experience with which some psychologists had identified it, his achievement in the area of religious studies would still be impressive.

## The Limits of Psychology

Psychology deals exclusively with the empirical aspect of experience, leaving out of consideration its *ideal* aspect. It ignores its intrinsic limitation when it claims to understand the religious act entirely by the genetic process or the psychic components of the experience. Such an interpretation never attains the religious consciousness as it is ideally related to a transcendent terminus. To "explain' the entire religious act psychologically is to reduce it to the non-religious, be it as an expression of fear, a projection of the father image, or as a sublimation of man's sexual drive. We should not be surprised to learn that with this approach religion turns out to be an illusion. But, as Scheler pointed out, the illusion here lies in the method itself.

The psychological processes which, as observed by introspection, are active within the praying subject, and the manner of their activity—these are matters as indifferent for the nature of the act of prayer as are a mathematician's indigestion or his fantasies, while he thinks a problem over, for the noetics of mathematics. The act of prayer can be defined only from the meaning of prayer.[1]

Still, if psychology is unable to explain why two plus two equals four, it can determine *how* a person reaches this conclusion and, even more importantly, *why* some people don't. Similarly, it may expose a particular religious experience as sham and it is thereby fully entitled to question the authenticity of the act itself. To accomplish this task the psychologist need not even possess a clear idea of what religion is in itself. It is sufficient that, within the limits of his science, he uncover the various emotional components in alleged religious phenomena. No act is ever "pure." All religious activity is determined by a person's psychic constitution insofar as the latter provides the necessary condition of the intentional act. In some instances this determination may change the nature of the act, as when a person under the cover of the religious act expresses emotions of an entirely different nature. In such a case the act can no longer be considered authentic, because its psychic determination prevents the intentionality from being what it pretends to be. But such a clear situation rarely occurs. Usually the religious act consists of a mixture of the hidden and the overt. It remains the difficult task of psychology to establish what ultimately motivates the agent.

Assuming, then, that empirical psychology deals with the real and phenomenology with the ideal, the question arises whether phenomenology itself is sufficiently equipped to provide an adequate explanation of the religious act. There seem to be at least two requirements for an understanding of the religious act which phenomenology, insofar as it remains pure phenomenology, is hard put to fulfill. One is the maintenance of the transcendence of the religious object; the other, the insistence on its real existence (over and above its intentional being).

## Transcendence of the Religious Object

The difficulty of the first requirement appears immediately. If the terminus of the religious act is transcendent, at least part of the act falls beyond description and can only be an object of faith. Yet the phenomenologist through his science claims to reach an intuition of what the religious act intends. Some phenomenologists treat this problem lightly. According to Scheler, God is revealed symbolically in the world and its structure, and man knows him in these symbols through a direct, non-rational intuition. In spite of all his insistence on the negative character of this insight, Scheler still seems to hold the possibility of a genuine *Wesensschau* of the divine. But such a position jeopardizes the transcendence of the religious terminus or it reduces phenomenological insight to an act of faith.

Van der Leeuw more cautiously distinguishes religion-as-experience from religion-as-transcendent. The former is a search for the meaning of life in its totality:

> But this meaning is never understood, this last word is never spoken; always they remain superior, the ultimate meaning being a secret which reveals itself repeatedly, only nevertheless to remain eternally concealed. It implies an advance to the farthest boundary, where only one sole fact is understood— that all comprehension is "beyond"; and thus the ultimate meaning is at the same moment the limit of meaning.[2]

The immanent experience, then, does not contain the transcendent as such which may be revealed but can never be a phenomenon. At most, religion-as-experience points toward the need for a revelation because of its own insufficiency. Phenomenology describes only this immanent reaching toward a transcendent and phenomenologically unknown being.

However, the religious act does not merely *reach* toward an unknown, as may appear to the outsider; it *attains* its transcendent object. But precisely because the object is transcendent, the act attains it only in faith. To the believer (and it is his experience which phenomenology describes) there is no distinction between an immanent reaching toward, and the attainment of, a transcendent reality. If a transcendent reality can only be an object of faith, it is also true that faith alone renders an object transcendent. No known reality is sacred in itself; only the attitude of faith determines it as sacred by subsuming it under its own intentionality. This holds for the Christian or Jew of our own age as well as for the primitive. Only the religious attitude constitutes the acts and words of Christ or the prophets into sacred history and sacred doctrine. But then the question becomes all the more urgent whether the object of faith does not fall altogether beyond the phenomenological *epoche*. Moreover, if the object falls beyond the scope of the phenomenologist's inquiry, the entire act which is specified by it becomes equally unknown.

To avoid such a conclusion, Van der Leeuw, who agrees that all religion is based on faith, distinguishes between theological faith (faith directly determined by a revelation) and the faith into which all understanding turns as soon as it realizes that the ground of understanding does not lie in itself but in some "other" all-comprehending being. Only the latter would be open to phenomenology. But even this distinction does not seem to be sufficient, for religious faith differs from any other form of belief in that it is directly specified by what the believer takes to be a transcendent revelation. It is always theological faith. Precisely because of this specification by its object, a correct understanding of the religious act cannot ignore altogether the revelation in which it originates. And such a revelation, by its very nature, falls beyond the reach of autonomous reflection.

One might answer that phenomenology may still consider the transcendent object *insofar as it enters into experience which intends it,* even though it must bracket the transcendent reality of that object which is not immanent in the conscious act as such. But can the phenomenological reflection comprehend the act and the object of faith without sharing its believing attitude? It is by no means clear how it can perform this abstraction. For the believing attitude enters into the very meaning of the religious assertion. A proposition held in faith essentially differs from the same proposition entertained outside faith. The doxic modality affects not only the real experience of the act but also its ideal object. Being part of the *ideal noesis* it definitely influences the understanding of the ideal *noema*. Consequently, to consider the latter outside the modality of faith is to miss its properly religious significance. On the other hand, to include the transcendent as such into the phenomenological investigation is to abandon the *epoche* and to transform phenomenological reflection into a reflection *within* faith, that is, into theology.

The difficulty here lies not in the relation between a detached phenomenological reflection and a live experience—a universal problem in an introspective act which by its very nature excludes that experience. No, it is quite unique to the reflection on the act of faith as such. For while other experiences bring their objects intentionally but fully within the immanence of consciousness, the act of faith achieves only a partial immanence. Though its transcendent object must become immanent for consciousness to *attain* it at all, it becomes immanent only by being experienced as *beyond attainment*. Its immanence consists in the very awareness of transcendence.

This severely limits a phenomenological analysis of the object of the religious act. In the act of faith the immanent being of consciousness, even in its purely ideal intentionality, can be grasped only in its *essential connection with the transcendent as such*. Since the establishment of that connection itself depends on an act of faith, any analysis of the act requires some sharing in that faith itself. It would seem, then, that no phenomenological reflection on the act of the faith is possible unless the phenomenologist adopts at least temporarily the believing attitude himself. Hence the phenomenological *epoche* cannot be consistently maintained in a reflection of this nature. According to Scheler the religious act cannot be understood at all without faith, that is, without an *actual acceptance* of the transcendent existence of its object.[3] Obviously, if this were entirely true a reflection on the act of faith would have to abandon all the restrictions of the phenomenological method. I suspect that Scheler was fully conscious of the import of his position but that he saw no other way for phenomenology to cope with the religious act than by radically expanding the phenomenological reflection.

However, other approaches to the transcendently real require less drastic modifications of the phenomenological method. Of particular interest here is how the father of phenomenology himself envisioned the question. Once asked by his disciple Roman Ingarden what he thought to be the fundamental problem in philosophy, Husserl replied: "The problem of God, of course." Yet, even though his writings raised a religious question which became more and more urgent in his later years, Husserl never attempted a methodic study of the "problem of God."

Why did he neglect to treat systematically a question which he considered to be so important? Perhaps because he thought of religion as the *final* problem, which must wait until all others have been dealt with. Thus he writes in a manuscript about the scientific understanding of religion:

> A great problem that can be solved only at the end of philosophy consists in the clarification of the symbolic process that takes place in religious symbols.[4]

### Husserl and the Transcendent Foundation of Consciousness

In Husserl the term transcendence usually refers to any being intended by consciousness whose reality falls outside consciousness. Thus the world "transcends" the mind insofar as it can never be exhaustively given in introspection, but must be revealed through an unending series of perspective variations. But the process of constitution itself involves transcendence since the object is not fully given with the nature of the constituting subject. The ability to constitute a world as basis of all scientific truth is itself a contingent fact that must be explained.

Husserl rejects idealism's ontological transition from the essence of consciousness to the necessary existence of the actual world. As he points out in his *Erste Philosophie*:

> Why must the laws of logic have a field of application? In a factual nature? Undoubtedly, transcendental logic as transcendentally related to consciousness contains the ground for a possible nature, but not for an actual one. . . . The astonishing fact here is the rationality which appears in an absolute consciousness that does not constitute just anything but a nature which is the correlate of a positive science of nature.[5]

The theological implications of this rationality are indicated in section 58 of *Ideen I* on the suspension of the transcendent being of God in the phenomenological *epoche*. The world reveals certain internal connections without which a scientific description would not be possible.

This very world, so far as its material basis is concerned, permits at once of being determined in the theoretical thought of the mathematically grounded natural sciences as the "appearance" of a *physical nature* that conforms to exact natural laws. And since *the rationality* which the fact-world shows is not in any sense such as the essence demands, there lies concealed in all this a wonderful teleology.[6]

The natural sciences are not able to account for this teleology in the particular aspects of nature which they study, much less for the teleology that gives coherence to the world as a whole. The question concerning the *ground* of the factual world constituted in consciousness is therefore legitimate and, insofar as this fact-world is the basis of all possible values, necessary.[7]

The world remains a contingent fact that is not fully explained by the nature of consciousness alone. Logically, its nonexistence is . not contradictory. Our present notion of the world is based upon a uniform perception which, we presume, will continue to present itself consistently in the future. But the possibility always exists that it will not, and even that perception will discontinue altogether. Since the idea of nonexistence can be brought to evident clarity, Husserl concludes that there is no apodictic necessity for the existence of the world. In the second part of the *Erste Philosophie* we read:

Every fact, and thus also the fact of the world, is qua fact *contingent*. This implies that it could be different from what it is and even that it could not be. . . . While I am aware of the world as a self-given, uninterrupted certainty, the existence of which I cannot doubt, this world still retains a continuous cognitive contingency in the sense that its bodily presence does not exclude in principle its non-being.[8]

It is true, consciousness *as it actually exists* could not be without a world. In that sense, we may refer to the existence of *a* world as a necessity of consciousness. But since consciousness itself is a contingent *fact*, it alone cannot provide a sufficient foundation for reality.[9] Such a foundation requires a necessary being and not merely the being of consciousness. In order to define its nature, we must first establish the contingency of consciousness itself.

Does consciousness itself need a transcendent foundation? This question is the same as: Could consciousness also not be? The individual consciousness is obviously not self-sufficient, for it requires the cooperation of other minds to reach objectivity. But could not the totality of all human minds which constitute the world as it is actually given to the individual be considered necessary? No, for even this empirical totality retains an element of arbitrariness. A different human race with different cultures would undoubtedly have constituted a different world. Of course, the transcendental subject which supports this empirical multisubjective community is definitely not contingent. The question is, however, whether it also provides its own foundation. Husserl's answer vacillates without ever reaching a final conclusion. Although his middle period was marked by strong idealistic tendencies, he nevertheless maintained in *Ideen* I that transcendental subjectivity is not an ultimate absolute.

The transcendental "Absolute" which we have laid bare through the reductions is in truth not ultimate: it is something which in a certain profound and wholly unique sense constitutes itself, and has its primeval source in what is ultimately and truly absolute.[10]

This text can be interpreted in two different ways. It is possible that Husserl here poses directly a theological problem. Such an interpretation connects the passage with the well-known section 58 of *Ideen* I in which the transcendence of God is declared to be "an 'Absolute' in a totally different sense from the absolute of consciousness, as on the other hand it would be transcendent in a totally different sense from the transcendent in the sense of the world."[11] A theological interpretation leaves us, however, with the difficult task of defining the relationship between the transcendental and the true, the ultimate absolute. If the transcendental absolute is not the ultimate absolute, how then can it be *given* as absolute? And how can a phenomenological reduction bracket the "transcendent absolute"? Or is this "reduction" merely a convenient abstraction, a leaving out of focus in Berkeley's sense, rather than a phenomenological reduction in the true sense of the word?[12]

A nontheological meaning could be given to the "truly absolute" on the basis of Husserl's *Phänomenologie des inneren Zeitbewusstseins*. Beyond the actual phenomena in time, and even beyond the time flow itself, is the time-constituting ego as the absolute source of consciousness. This constituting ego needs no further foundation, since it constitutes *itself* as well as all other temporal phenomena.[13] But even this interpretation raises theological problems. Does the self-constituting nature of the ego imply that it needs no further foundation? If so, how is it that we can still wonder what makes the ego self-constituting? To consider the constituting·activity itself an *ultimate* absolute is simply begging the question. For unless we find other evidence that the transcendental ego itself is an ultimate absolute or that its constituting activity is supported by some further, transcendent foundation, the constitution itself remains entirely contingent and may at any moment cease to exist. In a pre-existentialist text of 1923 on the postulates of Kant's *Critique of Practical Reason*, Husserl precisely envisages the case of a constituting activity that would have no necessary foundation.

What if the process of active and passive constitution and hence subjective life in the form of a human body related to a constituted environment *(Umwelt)* were a mere "chance"? Is it not better, in that case, to tell me: Life in the world is an illusion, aimless, without any outcome? In that event, I could not definitively accept life in society and in the world. Such an acceptance is possible only if I believe in the meaning of the world. But I have no "theoretical" grounds for doing that.[14]

Reflection upon the constituting activity of the ego will never yield the certitude that this activity is more than "chance." Only an ultimate absolute that entirely surpasses the constituting activity itself can provide such a much needed foundation. Husserl's half-expressed hope of finding this ultimate absolute as a postulate of moral action is hereby less important than his admission that the constituting ego needs a further foundation at all. It is precisely his awareness of this insufficiency which leads him in later years to explore the idea of a universal teleology directing the activity of the time-constituting ego. In a manuscript of 1933 he states:

In my former doctrine of internal consciousness I treated the thereby-discovered intentionality simply as intentionality: directed toward the future as protention, and modified yet still preserving its unity as retention; but I did not mention the ego, I did not characterize the intentionality of the self (intentionality of the will in the broadest sense). Later, I introduced the latter as founded in an egoless ("passivity"). But is not the ego of the acts and of the act-habits which originate in them, in development itself? May we not, or must we not presuppose a universal intentional drive which unifies each original present into a lasting temporalization [stehende Zeitung einheitlich ausmacht] and which propels it concretely from present to present in such a way that each content is content of a fulfilled drive?[15]

In Husserl's later writings, it is precisely this forward moving force of an all-comprehensive, teleological principle which secures the unified, homogeneous character of the inner time flow. As ordering principle of a dynamic universal harmony, this teleological "ultimate" proceeds from preconscious life through animal and subconscious awareness to full conscious monads directing them toward the constitution of one common, objective world. According to this view, all intentionality of consciousness is founded in a transconscious universal drive.[16]

Husserl refers to this subjacent intentionality as an "open infinity" because he assumes that the universal teleology, although revealed in the finite mind, is directed toward an infinite perfection. Such an infinite ideal cannot but transcend time-constituted consciousness, which is by its very nature finite-bound. "All that is attainable is finite, all being qua temporal lies in the finite order and is merely on its way to infinity—that is, under the idea of absolute perfection."[17]

Without an infinite, transcendent *telos*, the forward-moving, universal intentionality would come to a halt within temporally constituted being. In that case, the process of reason would lead literally nowhere. Rather than accepting the possibility of such an aimless intentionality, Husserl assumes that to all finite, temporally constituted being corresponds infinite being as "an idea giving all relative being in the totality of time *(Allzeitlichkeit)* its meaning of being."[18]

The importance of the notion of teleology in Husserl's later writings is probably due to the increasing influence of Fichte's work. Husserl had been acquainted with his work for some time. During World War I, he had delivered three popular lectures on Fichte's ethical ideal of man. These ethical considerations made him aware of the universal import of the notion of teleology. All finite ends of action are connected in an ultimate *telos*.[19] This ultimate *telos* determines the entire activity of the transcendental subject, for all acting is driven by a desire for "what alone can exist as an end in itself, what alone has in itself an absolute value."[20] For Fichte this ideal is ethical, for moral action alone, and nothing else in the world, has absolute value. The moral order then, is the end of man, and, through him, of the world.[21]

Over the years, Husserl came more and more under the influence of Fichte. In a text written between 1930 and 1934 he describes how man is constantly striving to achieve a perfect world. This ideal world is the infinite *telos* which guides him in constituting the world of experience.[22] The question, however, is whether this infinite *telos* is transcendent. Husserl himself seems to consider it as that which gives a transcendent dimension to man's ethical striving. The important manuscript E 111 4 describes the ethical ideal as an absolute "that far surpasses the transcendental subject." It adds:

This ideal itself is only a ray of the absolute ideal, of the ideal of an all-person that infinitely transcends all contingency *(das*

*Faktische)* as well as all becoming and all development of the contingent toward the idea; it is a pole which lies infinitely far beyond it; it is the idea of an absolutely perfect transcendental total community.[23]

This description certainly conveys the idea of transcendence. In addition, Husserl's ideal is infinite: it gives all relative, finite striving its meaning. Husserl himself does not hesitate to refer to it as "God."[24] But it is hard to say whether he has in mind the absolutely transcendent, personal Being for whom religion reserves the name "God."

The infinite *telos* unquestionably transcends each single individual time-constituted being. But does it also transcend the totality of temporal being? The above-quoted text could undoubtedly be interpreted in a strictly theistic sense. However, other texts of the same period are less clear and could apply to an immanent *telos*. In Manuscript E III 9, for instance, Husserl declares that through transcendental being the transcendent *telos* realizes its ideal design and "creates" a world. This creating, we should add, is not a full *creatio ex nihilo* but rather a redemption of the world from its inner conflict between being and nonbeing. It brings it to full objectivity.[25] The text is sufficiently obscure to be ambiguous, but the following passage can hardly be interpreted in any but a purely immanent way:

So we understand the absolute teleology which is the correlate of the inseparable unity of all finite beings as merely dependent moments in the "infinite" unity of meaning in a meaning-giving process that moves into infinity, and again this teleology can be understood in its relation to the absolute subjectivity as the infinite way along which it moves toward its true being.[26]

If the infinite *telos* is not more than the immanent force that moves the absolute subjectivity, it can hardly be termed "transcendent" in the strict sense. Even the unbridgeable distance separating the ideal from man's actual achievements does not make it "divine" in the usual, absolutely transcendent sense of the word. For the fact that this ideal is partly realized excludes it from being an adequate concept of a transcendent God. That Husserl had such a "realization" in mind appears clearly enough from a manuscript of 1931 which discusses man's contribution to the process of God's "self-realization."[27] The difficulty with a teleological approach to the problem of God is that it quite naturally makes the *telos* an immanent part of the teleological movement itself. Another difficulty lies in the phenomenological method itself, which recognizes only *constituted* being (phenomena) and *constituting* being (transcendental subjectivity), neither one of which can accommodate the idea of a transcendent God.

All the more remarkable is it that Husserl, in spite of his method, strives to attain a purely transcendent *telos*. The same manuscript that seems to jeopardize the notion of transcendence altogether refers to God as *Überwahrheit, Überwirklichkeit, Über-an-sich*.[28] God is called an *idea* and compared to Plato's idea of the good that lies beyond all being and without which no being is possible. The term *idea* in itself is well chosen, for, as Strasser remarks, an idea is neither constituting nor constituted. "It is that which gives the constituting activities unity, meaningful coherence and teleology. It is no mundane being and still a 'final, absolute reality.' "[29] Even so, Husserl is not fully satisfied and denies that Plato's idea is sufficiently *ideal* to apply to God.[30] Is this because Plato's idea is still object of a possible intuition, whereas Husserl's idea of God lies beyond all experience?[31] Or is it because no Platonic idea, not even the idea of the good, may rightly be called absolute? Husserl writes:

> [There is] only one Logos of truth, only one God who is an idea that implies its own ontological uniqueness, a being *(Wesen)* that is not *eidos* but being *(Wesen)* in absolute truth, a being that is in no relativity of situation, in no horizontality but that, because it carries all true being in absolute necessity, is alone and real—real in the sense of a superreality which founds and makes possible all reality of every relative, every finite bearer of meanings.[32]

The reason why Husserl is so concerned about finding a true transcendence is that the teleological process itself contains too much contingency to account for its own being. The true absolute, however, must provide its own foundation.

> The absolute has its ground in itself and in its groundless being its absolute necessity as the one "absolute existence." Its necessity is not a necessity of being which still admits contingency.[33]

We now see that the problem of transcendence on the part of the subject is ultimately one of contingency—not of teleology. Teleology has merely broadened the problem of contingency. It has not solved it. For, with respect to the absolute, all depends on whether a teleological process has its ground in itself or in another being. This resurrects the problem of causality, since it is hard to see how the contingent could have its ground in the necessary without standing in some sort of causal relation to it. Unfortunately, by refusing to consider the problem from any other than a teleological viewpoint, Husserl has made it impossible to solve it at all. As long as a *purely* teleological viewpoint is maintained, the *telos* can never become independent of the teleological process itself. Even when Husserl defines the *telos* of transcendental subjectivity as purely ideal and thus beyond any actual "realization," he nonetheless conceives it exclusively in terms of transcendental subjectivity. The following description of a "purely ideal *telos*" illustrates this point.

> This ideal of the concretely constituting transcendental subjectivity is not and will never be in time, as actual transcendental subjectivity is. This *idea*, even though it is the idea of a temporally "absolutely perfect" intersubjective community, lies entirely in infinity.[34]

So the basic question still remains: Is the absolute *more* than an infinite *telos* for consciousness? It is described as the ideal *of consciousness*, but is it essentially *different from* consciousness? Even the causal problem cannot be avoided altogether. Husserl himself wonders what has led consciousness itself out of the dark origins of the preconscious. What is at the root of the teleological process? Husserl feels unable to answer these questions. His most fundamental passage on the absolute ideal concludes with the following query:

Is it necessary that this ideal, founded in such absoluteness, should have led and should lead the evolution of the world? In prehistory as an obscure evolutionary impetus, as instinctive intentionality, later in the clear consciousness of authentic humanity (now in the sense of a human race that has opted for this ideal)?[35]

The transcendence of Husserl's "infinite *telos*" becomes even more questionable in his last years when he leans more and more toward a philosophy of the *spirit*.[36] This final deveiopment of Husserl's thought may have widened his philosophical horizon (particularly by giving his thinking a historical dimension), but at the same time it abrogated whatever transcendence his notion of the absolute had contained. The *spirit* of the German idealist tradition is both all-comprehensive and self-sufficient. As Husserl said at a lecture on the crisis in Western science held on May 10, 1935 in Vienna:

In a reflection on the spirit as spirit, there is no reason to require any other than a purely spiritual interpretation. . . . Blinded by naturalism (however much they fight it in words), the natural scientists have neglected even to pose the problem of a universal and pure science of the spirit.[37]

It is true that this text is directed against naturalism and positivism. But it implies much more than a simple rejection of naturalism, for such a rejection by itself does not lead to a "universal science of the spirit." Husserl fought naturalism all his life, yet it is only toward the end that he accepted a philosophy of the spirit. In such a philosophy consciousness must be its own foundation. Actual, *empirical* consciousness may be contingent, but transcendental subjectivity *as such* is self-sufficient and necessary. No theism, however, could accept a God who is identical with transcendental subjectivity or even one who needs it as an essential part of himself. From this point of view, Husserl's later philosophy is perhaps even further removed from a true transcendence than his earlier. A strange observation in view of the fact that his personal convictions became increasingly theistic![38]

We may conclude that the transcendent character of Husserl's absolute remains doubtful. If it can be established at all, it is through contingency rather than teleology. Least of all did Husserl ever prove the existence of a *personal* transcendent being. This, he felt, was entirely a matter of faith. It would be mistaken, however, to conclude that religious problems are therefore of no concern to the *philosopher* Husserl. His attitude must rather be viewed as related to that of Kant, who replaced the philosophical knowledge of God by *faith*, that is, a firm belief in the ultimate meaningfulness of existence beyond the point where this meaning can be proven or even easily accepted.

> Man lives by faith and that is precisely why he lives in a world that has meaning for him and which he constantly accepts to the extent that he, as a religious subject, does justice to it. Correlatively with this, his life, his existence in the world has meaning to him; he cannot give himself up or give up the world that stands under the idea of religion—precisely because he constantly negates the evil in himself and outside himself as that for which he recognizes to be co-responsible.[39]

Faith for Husserl is belief in teleology. A teleological view of being is one that grasps reality in its organic totality. But such a view reaches beyond all finite horizons and, as Kant had pointed out, is no longer rational insight but belief.[40] "In faith we experience the teleology that directs us, that rules through sin and error as a lasting, self-preserving disposition which gives fulfilment."[41]

For Husserl, the connection between faith and teleology is essential. Religion ultimately arises out of the need for a total understanding of existence. The salvation it offers consists in the bestowal of meaning upon those purely contingent and unnecessary events which are the warp and woof of life and the despair of speculative reason. But the redeeming insight of faith is given to man only as he turns into himself.

In this reflection of man on his destiny [in dieser Innen-wendung des Menschen im Schicksal] originates the religious evidence of the saving God who is not a theorem but the one who redeems us from the bonds of the world (not the world in the scientific sense), who restores the ego's existence to truth and authenticity, who leads us into true freedom.[42]

Theoretical reason can never justify the proposition that life is wholly meaningful.[43] Yet, the acceptance of this proposition is necessarily postulated by man's ethical striving. Religious faith alone then provides the foundation of morality.[44] Husserl's interpretation is obviously influenced by Kant's theory of the postulates of practical reason, to which he refers repeatedly.[45] However, Husserl disagrees with Kant insofar as the infinite teleology is somehow *directly experienced* by the religious mind.

## NOTES

1. Max Scheler, *On the Eternal in Man* (New York: Harper, 1960), p. 155.
2. *Religion in Essence and Manifestation* (New York: Harper, 1959), p. 680.
3. *On the Eternal in Man*, p. 261.
4. E III 9, p. 30.
Most of the relevant material was never published by Husserl and had to be found in the manuscripts of the Husserl Archives. Translations of the manuscripts are the author's own and follow the numerals of the manuscripts at the Husserl Archives in Louvain. Most of these manuscripts consist of private annotations jotted down as "thinking-aids" without any intention of future publication. Their unpolished character precludes an elegant translation.
5. *Erste Philosophie*, II, Husserliana VIII, The Hague, 1959, Beilage 20, p. 394. This text is quoted by Kern.
6. *Ideen* I, Husserliana III, The Hague, 1950, p. 139. Translation W. R. Boyce Gibson (London, 1958), p. 174.
7. This question is not pursued any further in *Ideen* I, which deals only with the "absolute" being of consciousness and not with the absolute ground of all being. Husserl merely remarks: "What concerns us here, after this simple reference to the various groups of such rational motives indicating the existence of a 'divine' being beyond the world, is that such a being transcends not only the world, but also the 'absolute' consciousness." (*Ideen* I, p. 139-40. My translation.)

8. *Erste Philosophie*, II, Husserliana VIII, p. 50. See also p. 392 (Erganzende Texte).

9. Kern exactly captures the trend of Husserl's thought in the following paradox: "Transcendental subjectivity "produces" the transcendent world; yet, it does not possess this "production" as its own power, but as one which constantly receives. Mindful of the terminological nuances we may say: According to Husserl, subjectivity "produces" the world, but does not "create" it. That is why the world retains also for subjectivity an insurmountable aspect of strangeness. In the facticity of the constitution of the world, that is, in the impossibility to explain it from the transcendental subjectivity, Husserl saw the starting-point of metaphysics proper." Iso Kern, *Kant und Husserl. Phenomenologica* 16, The Hague, 1964, p. 298.

10. *Ideen* I, Husserliana III, p. 198. Gibson p. 236.

11. *Ibid*, p. 140. Gibson p. 174. This interpretation has been adopted by Rudolf Boehm in "Zum Bergiff des 'Absoluten' bei Husserl" in *Zeitschrift für philosophische Forschung* 13 (1959), pp. 240-241.

12. Boehm, *art. cit.*, p. 240.

13. *Phanomenologie des inneren Zeitbewusstseins*, Husserliana X, The Hague, 1966.

14. *Erste Philosophie*, II, Appendix, Husserliana VIII, pp. 354-355.

15. E III 5, pp. 3-4. I am unsure of the translation of the German text which is added in brackets.

16. E III 9, p. 66.

17. E III 9, p. 26.

18. E III 4, p. 31.

19. F I 22, p. 20.

20. F I 22, p. 24.

21. Interestingly enough, Husserl at the end of his lectures describes how Fichte abandons teleological considerations as an insufficient foundation for a religious attitude. "In Fichte's *Vocation of Man*," he remarks, "the ethical and the religious are no longer identified as they were in previous works. God, then, is no longer the *ordo ordinans* but the infinite *will*, as it is called here, that causes *(bewirkt)* this order in the first place. He is the *creator of the world* in the finite mind. It is his light through which we see all light and all that appears to us in this light." See F I 22, p. 35-36.

This text marks a return to a causal relationship between God and the world through *the finite mind*. Yet it is certainly not the causal relationship between God and the world of traditional philosophy. Husserl's own thought on this problem in his later period will take a somewhat similar turn.

22. E III 1, p. 3.

23. E III 4, p. 61.

24. E III 4, p. 64.

25. "The world is and is not, insofar as it is always in relatively true

being and in relative nonbeing. And this again can be understood differently insofar as the world which is not fully awake yet, which is not clearly aware of truth and falsity may indeed be referred to as nonbeing, as not even relative being yet. The world is constantly being created from nothing because its true being consists in the progress of the degrees of being which are degrees of relativity. Being here has the meaning of transcendental being." E III 9, pp. 65-66.

26. E III 4, p. 60.

27. A V 22, p. 46. According to one recent commentator this means: "God is the idea in us toward which I strive in my life and which I help to realize. As teleological idea God is bound to my subjective a priori; he receives a sense of being only through my positing a sense of being." Hubert Hohl, *Lebenswelt und Geschichte*, Freiburg, 1962, p. 86.

28. E III 4, p. 62.

29. Stephan Strasser, "Das Gottesproblem in der Spätphilosophie Edmund Husserls," in *Philosophisches Jahrbuch* 67, p. 141. This excellent article was later reprinted in a collection of Strasser's essays, *Bouwstenen voor een filosofische anthropologie*, Hilversum-Antwerpen, 1965, pp. 293-311.

30. F I 14, pp. 43, 66.

31. Strasser, art. cit., p. 142.

32. E III 4, p. 62.

33. E III 9, p. 75.

34. E III 1, p. 4. Immediately after this passage, Husserl even implies that the *ideal* remains unattainable only because of some basic sinfulness inherent to human nature, as if man in a more innocent state of mind would have been able to actualize this infinite ideal.

35. E III 1, p. 7.

36. See Strasser, *art. cit.*, pp. 132-134.

37. *Die Krisis der Europeischen Wissenschaften und die transzendentale Phänomenologie*, Abhandlungen, Husserliana VI, The Hague, 1962, pp. 317-318. This lecture varies substantially from the one held in Prague on the same topic.

38. See H. L. Van Breda, "Husserl et le problème de Dieu" in *Proceedings of the 10th International Congress of Philosophy*, Amsterdam (1949), pp. 1210-1212.

39. E III 4, p. 47.

40. E III 4, p. 50.

41. E III 10, p. 21.

42. E III 4, p. 56.

43. E III 1, p. 8.

44. A V 21, p. 9.

45. He writes somewhere that this theory is Kant's main contribution to philosophy!

# 5
# Blondel's Reflection on Experience

Religion obviously cannot be understood by a philosophy which *a priori* denies the very possibility of a relation between the human mind and a transcendent reality. Yet, equally unfit is the "gnostic" philosophy which, all too confidently, incorporates the transcendent into its own immanent schemes of thought. The believer is right in distrusting such an approach as lacking in intellectual integrity. In the study of religion the philosopher must acquire the delicate skill of remaining both sufficiently open to the transcendent as to admit its presence in ways which he cannot fully comprehend, and sufficiently autonomous as to explain no more than his method allows.

### The Immanent and the Transcendent

Maurice Blondel fully understood that philosophy of religion must maintain its independence with regard to faith, while at the same time it must establish at least the possibility of a transcendent reality. He therefore began his philosophical work by showing how the human act is essentially directed toward a transcendent goal. Blondel thus attempted to establish the possibility—but no more than the possibility—of a revealed religion. But there is more. Since the task of philosophy is to reflect on the phenomena of consciousness in order to discover their fundamental structure, and since religion consists, at least partly, of conscious phenomena, philosophy must reflect upon religious as well as upon all other phenomena.

The essential characteristic of revealed religion is transcendence but philosophy is by its very nature restricted to the study of immanent structures. The transcendent nature of revealed religion appears to preclude any philosophical assertion of its existence. Philosophy's difficulty with a "supernatural" order lies not so much in the content of this order, for if this content is to be assimilated by the mind, it must conform to the laws of the mind and fit its immanent structure. Not *what* man believes, but that his belief requires a *transcendent* order of reality, is the crux of the philosophical problem. Applying this to Christianity, Blondel writes:

> Even if (by an impossible hypothesis) we would discover, by a stroke of genius, almost the entire wording and content of revealed doctrine, we still would possess nothing, absolutely nothing of the Christian spirit, because it is not ours. Not to have it as received and given to us, but as discovered and originating in ourselves is not to have it at all; and that is precisely the scandal of reason.[1]

In his early writings Blondel shows how philosophy can actually consider the transcendent reality of religion without abandoning its own immanent method.[2] Philosophy, he admits, can never discover the transcendent order as a *reality*, for such a discovery would *eo ipso* abolish its transcendence. Yet, even though as an *actual reality* the supernatural falls entirely beyond the scope of immanent reflection, as a *necessary* hypothesis it constitutes an essential part of an immanent philosophy. *L'Action* shows how, in the dialectic of action, the free subject is inevitably confronted with the supernatural hypothesis. The *Letter on Apologetics* discusses to what extent philosophy is able, without abandoning its immanent autonomy, to analyze the structure of religion in its concrete, historical appearance.

## The Dialectic of Action

In *L'action* Blondel considers the human act in its totality, prior to its specification into appetitive and cognitive functions.

Experience shows that these functions have a common source: intelligence enlightens the will while the will propels the process of thinking. Both functions are united in the acting subject. Although this subject is the ultimate principle of action, its role is usually neglected. The positive sciences, for example, fail to distinguish what is *given* in the known object from what is actively *constituted* by the knowing subject. Yet, the part of the acting subject must be defined in any fundamental justification of the method of science. How could mathematical determination be combined with descriptive observation if both were not essentially related?

Now to Blondel this subjective element is not a conclusion of abstract speculation. It *appears* in the very unity which underlies all objective structures.

In reflecting upon the development of the exact sciences and the stages of their abstract constructions, one notices that they bring into their successful synthesis an ever increasing element of subjective ideality.[3]

No constitution, no formation of objective phenomena is possible without the subjective *act*. All-important in the study of phenomena, then, becomes what Blondel calls *le fait psychologique*.

The phenomenon is what it is in function of the activity which contributes to its production; one perceives it only in the order of its production and the constituting act of the subject is thereby essential.[4]

One may consider every phenomenon as determined by all others, but there always remains an irreducible surplus which makes the synthesis surpass the elements of which it is composed. The subjective act is conditioned by objective elements. Yet, no exhaustive knowledge of these objective elements can adequately define the act, because it always exceeds the sum of its conditions.[5] The subjective is not merely one element among others in the structure of the phenomenon. It is the *act which produces* the phenomenon, rather than a phenomenon itself. This brings us to the most essential feature of the acting subject: it is freedom *in act*.

But even as the constituting subject cannot be detached from the objective phenomena which it constitutes, freedom never appears independently of a system of determinations. It originates in determinism and results in a new determinism.

However, freedom always transcends its determinations: it introduces an element which gives these determinations a new weight and function. No deliberate motive is possible without a natural impulse of desire, but in the clear motive of the act, the impulse attains a firmness and a precision which it did not possess of itself. "The entire impact of the impulses *(mobiles)* comes from the motive which they prepare and propose."[6] The motive always transcends the impulse which conditions it; it assumes all preceding energies and utilizes them for the attainment of an end which lies beyond these energies. Far from being the opposite of freedom, then, determinism is an essential part of it. It is the condition which freedom transforms into its own determination by rendering blind instinct into clear motive.

Every choice of an external object seems to estrange the acting subject from itself. But such is precisely the nature of freedom that it can choose itself only by bestowing its own ideal character upon an extraneous object. Freedom progresses in a dialectical way: only while constantly losing itself does it find itself. In all its objects, freedom ultimately chooses itself or, rather, it chooses to transcend itself. This self-*transcendence*, which is the very heart of freedom, is expressed in the ascent from one determination to another.

As much as antecedent determinism proved indispensable to the manifestation of the free will, consequent determinism is an integral condition of freedom.[7]

In its constant self-expression, freedom penetrates the deterministic world of facts and reshapes it in accordance with its own spiritual intentions.

Thus the sign which expresses to the outside the moving drive [of the will] is at least the initial stage of a conquering invasion and of an absorption of the universe by the will.[8]

Every act of freedom synthesizes the total impulse of the mind.

However, living action *(l'action voulante)* always surpasses its accomplishments *(l'action voulue)*. The more freedom conquers, the more it becomes aware of its insufficiency and of its desire to terminate in an absolute, beyond the chain of phenomena. Its impetus attains only phenomena, but it increasingly *postulates* a transphenomenal reality. The *elan* of action always tends far beyond its actual and, indeed, beyond its possible achievements.

All attempts to bring human action to completion fail, and yet human action cannot but strive to complete itself and to suffice to itself. It must but it cannot.[9]

The feeling of impotence as well as the need for an infinite consummation remains incurable. The impetus which drives the will beyond all finite goals reveals an infinity in the very heart of action. This infinity is never present as an actual realization—it remains an exigency. But the exigency itself is eminently real: it keeps the need to achieve alive after the long expected fulfillment, as well as after constant disappointment. Although this exigency of transcendence appears primarily as a negation, since it has no place among the phenomena, its necessity constitutes the very foundation of all contingent action. And again, this necessity is not the conclusion of a speculative argument demonstrating that contingency cannot exist by itself; it *appears* in the contingent itself.

The same experience may be expressed in teleological terms. Action reveals an insurmountable discrepancy between the ideal and the real. The ideal surpasses the real but, in a sense, the real also surpasses the ideal. Thought precedes practice and practice precedes thought in what Blondel calls "une mutuelle et alternante propulsion de l'idée et de l'action."[10] The two never coincide. Yet, only if the two poles of action are united in an actual identity of the ideal and the real, is the mutual propulsion of imperfect action possible. In some form the ultimate identity must be present in the imperfect agent to enable him to act at all. Far from being a mere projection of his aspirations, it occupies the center of his actual thought and action, and allows him to proceed from thought to action and from action to thought. At the same time, the agent can never fully identify himself with it: its impact is revealed in the imperfection of his action as that power which allows him to continue his action in spite of its imperfection.

Blondel therefrom concludes, somewhat hastily perhaps, that in the very insufficiency of his action the finite agent finds God. Whether this reformulation of the arguments of contingency and design for the existence of God is valid or not, I shall not consider here. But in any event the argument leads beyond the purely phenomenal order. Indeed, Blondel considers his own descriptive analysis closer to the *reality* of the transcendent than the traditional speculative arguments.

> A proof which is merely a logical argument always remains abstract and partial; it does not lead to being; it does not compel thought to the real necessity. But a proof which results from the total movement of life, a proof which is action in its totality, has this compelling force.[11]

Blondel's argument follows in reflection the living movement of action. To be sure, the argument never "produces" reality: it makes no ontological transition from an ideal structure to a living reality. But it certainly deals with reality in describing a real movement from its real start to its real end. In fact, it does much more than describing, for it searches the *foundations* of the phenomena of consciousness, and *interprets* what appears in the phenomena themselves. It discovers the *necessity* of what is merely *given* in the original experience, by finding the structure of its internal determinations.

### The Problem of the Supernatural

I have emphasized the ontological and dialectical aspects of Blondel's thought on purpose, because a few passages in the *Letter* describe the distinction between reflection and living experience in terms which seem to exclude any direct reference to reality from his philosophy. That Blondel's so-called immanent method does not entail such a restriction appears from the preceding argument. The *Letter* itself describes his method in ontological terms:

> Philosophy's function is to determine the content of thought and the postulates of action; but it never provides *the being of which it studies the notion*, it never contains the life of which it analyzes the requirements, it never realizes that of which it must say that it necessarily conceives it as real.[12]

Philosophy, though it does not produce being itself, is certainly not restricted to a study of logical possibilities. In fact, its task is primarily to discover the necessary *in the real*. The limits which the *Letter* sets to philosophy with regard to the reality of a "supernatural" order are imposed by the special character of the revelation, not by philosophy's inability to deal with existence. If there is an ontological problem in *L'action*, it would rather be that its philosophy deals with more reality than it can handle. Indeed, the question has been raised whether the active presence of a transcendent terminus in all human action does not entail the *necessity* of a self-communication of this transcendent. Of course, *per se* the notion of God's existence does not imply the existence of a supernatural order. But if human action postulates an absolute beyond the chain of moral phenomena, because of the discrepancy between the basic impulse of the will and its actual realization, is this absolute, then, not *bound* to overcome the discrepancy through which it was discovered. "Human action cannot but seek self-completion and sufficiency. It needs both and yet it cannot achieve them."[13] But can the transcendent be manifest in a need without necessarily satisfying it? On the answer to this question ultimately depends the gratuitous, and therefore the genuinely transcendent, character of Blondel's supernatural. A lack of precision in Blondel's expression makes it easy enough to consider the *satisfaction of the need* a natural necessity. Yet, a closer look will reveal that the discovery of the transcendent in the very deficiency of action entails only the *possibility* (albeit a necessary one) of a transcendent fulfillment. Action naturally tends toward its completion, yet it is totally unable to reach this completion by itself. The transcendent is discovered exclusively in the *existing insufficiency*—not in the necessity of fulfillment.

Once the existence of a transcendent end has been posited,

it is logical enough to consider the *possibility* of a transcendent completion of human action. Yet, far from being a necessity, such a supernatural intervention raises new questions. How can I accept a thought other than my own, a life different from my own? And assuming that I am able to do this, how can that which is so much beyond my comprehension that it must be revealed, ever have a salvific effect upon my action? These questions are so difficult to answer that the possibility of a supernatural revelation would not occupy the philosopher's mind very long, were it not for religion's claim that this possibility has *actually* been realized. The analysis of human action leads the philosopher to the point where he *must* consider the claims of living religion. But it is equally certain that nature alone is unable to bring its essential aspirations to fulfillment.

> There is an infinity present to all our voluntary acts and this infinity cannot be contained in reflection or reproduced by human effort. If we are to grasp and produce this secret principle of all action, as we want to, then it must give itself to us in a form which allows us to enter into communion with it.[14]

This hypothesis is by no means arbitrary—it is necessary in the dialectic of action. Yet, its necessity is not an absolute one, the opposite of which would imply a contradiction. It is necessary only to consider the hypothesis—not to accept its realization. It is a necessity imposed by an awareness of insufficiency in all human action and the intrinsic need for its completion.[15] The idea is necessary as part of an ideal structure which philosophy must scrutinize if it is to justify the ground of human action at all.[16]

The existence of a supernatural order of reality in which man partakes remains entirely gratuitous in Blondel's thought. It is not implied in the existence of the absolute ground of action nor is it inherent in the living experience of action. Transcendence can be experienced in the insufficiency of action, but the existence of a supernatural order cannot. What religious man *experiences*—the symbols, sacred language, psychological effects and so forth—is not properly supernatural, but is rather that through which the transcendent communicates with the immanent.

The real problem raised by a supernatural order lying beyond all actual experience is: How can philosophy deal with it at all? Philosophy can never reflect upon an *existence* which is not given or logically implied by experience. Now, the existence of a transcendent terminus is implied in the living experience of action. But not the existence of any supernatural relation to that terminus, for precisely insofar as it is experienced, the relation is not experienced as supernatural. Experience is of itself immanent and, to the extent that the supernatural is reflected in conscious activity, it becomes part of a natural order and is subject to natural determinations. How can the believer *experience* the word of God as intrinsically different from the word of man? The sacred books are written in human language and use the symbols of a particular civilization in the evolution of man. The same holds true for their content: the events and meanings of sacred history relate to a totality of *human* experience and take their place in this totality. One may consider the preachings of Christ infinitely superior to any other religious or moral doctrine and still not accept their supernatural origin. The ideas of the sacred books can be compared with profane philosophies, from which they are often derived. Christ always appeared as a man. His divinity—and divine authority alone makes his message supernatural—can only be believed. Even miracles do not provide an *experience* of the divine: as events they take place in this world, much as they appear to conflict with the known laws of nature.

> If you go to the heart of the matter, there is not more in a miracle than in the smallest, ordinary event. . . . Miracles are miraculous only in the eyes of those who are already prepared to recognize God's activity in the most common events and acts.[17]

There can be no reflection upon the "supernatural experience" because there can be no experience of the supernatural *as such*. To some extent we may experience *transcendence* insofar as the immanent points beyond itself. But of the *supernatural* we can only experience the possibility. According to Blondel, this possibility is one which the philosopher *must* consider. Yet, no amount of reflection can ever transform it into an actuality. Faith alone can gain entrance to a supernatural reality, but faith itself is ultimately supernatural and, in that respect, beyond experience. The paradox of faith is precisely that it affirms more than it can experience and that the affirmation itself, insofar as it is supernatural, lies beyond experience.

## The Hypothetical Character of Reflection

Still, philosophy must consider the supernatural as possibility. It must analyze the intrinsic structure and the coherence of this hypothesis. But however philosophy of religion may go about this task, it must never leave the hypothetical plane. For if it were to commit itself existentially to a supernatural order, philosophy would become theology. No living faith or actual adherence to religious dogmas, therefore, can ever be required from the philosopher, however necessary a personal acquaintance with the religious experience (that is, the immanent part of religious faith) may be. It is precisely in order to remain within the methodological limits of his science that the philosopher must study the supernatural as a mere *possibility*. This restrictive attitude is by no means artificial or schizophrenic on the part of the believing philosopher. It merely keeps him aware of the fact that the supernatural order in which he believes is not an immanent necessity, and that the immanent structure on which he reflects provides no support to a supernatural interpretation of it. As a philosopher he may discern a transcendent reality in the structure of the immanent, but he cannot attain the reality of living dialogue with this transcendent, for such a reality forms no part of the immanent structure of the real.

Nor should the believer object to the noncommittal attitude of philosophy, for it is inspired by a profound respect for the nature of the transcendent. It does not negate or question the transcendent dimension of immanent affirmations; it only abstains from any statements which go beyond what is the proper area of philosophy—the immanent and the *immanent* references to the transcendent.

Again, this is not to say that philosophy must always abstain from asserting the real, but only that, because of the transcendent character of the supernatural, philosophy here must restrict itself to the possible. Even the existence of the transcendent can be philosophically asserted, for that existence is entailed by the immanent structure of consciousness itself. In the *Letter* Blondel discusses exclusively the supernatural and this accounts for the fact that the "immanent method" here may appear to exclude *any* reference to actual existence. True enough, philosophy can never be a substitute for living experience and, in the words of Henry Duméry, it does not participate in the ontogenetic process, but this is no reason why the road to ontology (that is, to the understanding of existence) should be closed. At times Blondel seems to have extended the unique, non-existential character of reflection upon the supernatural to all reflection. He then reserves the entire domain of existence to the living experience, and restricts all philosophical reflection to the merely possible. Duméry, Blondel's most perceptive commentator, interprets Blondel's immanent method in this restrictive way, where he writes: "On the level of representations (that is, of critical reflection), the philosopher deals exclusively with possibilities, even if these reveal themselves later as realities on the level of effective freedom."[18]

But, as the ontological affirmations of *L'Action* clearly demonstrate, the immanent method does not abstain from existential judgments. To do so would exclude ontology from the realm of philosophy and divorce the ideal from the real. Pure phenomenalism[19] then could be avoided only by an acceptance of the rationalist presupposition that the ideal order runs *parallel* with the real, because they are ultimately identical. It is obvious from *L'action* and his later works that Blondel would have rejected such a position, but it may well be that he inherited his fascination with "the possible" from Leibnitz who influenced him more than any other philosopher. Blondel never accepted Leibnitz's rationalism, but I do not see how, without it, a non-existential philosophy can escape phenomenalism.

Moreover, from a religious point of view, the distinction between immanent reflection and living experience seems to replace, or at least to obscure, the more essential distinction between the transcendent and the immanent. Blondel's *Letter* gives the impression that the supernatural *reality* falls beyond the scope of philosophical reflection, *because* it belongs to the living experience. But this implies that the supernatural *can* be experienced—which would render it immanent. One cannot but agree with Blondel's statement that "concrete thought and lived life surpass our immanent knowledge, even of the transcendent and even of the supernatural." Yet, one feels, the emphasis has shifted from the more important distinction between immanent and transcendent to the less important one between living experience and reflection.

This anti-ontological trend in Blondel's thinking appears quite clearly in his criticism of the ancient concept of philosophy which "enveloped the entire order of thought and reality." The reason why the philosophy of the Middle Ages failed in its relations with religion is, in his opinion, that it adopted the rationalism of the Ancients. Since Christianity is essentially opposed to the deification of reason, the subject matter of medieval philosophy no longer fitted the ancient form and could only produce a hybrid. Modern philosophy, according to Blondel, has become more modest in its aims.

It no longer takes knowledge for a complete substitute of effective existence; . . . thought is insufficient to bring us on a level with ourselves or with reality.[20]

Applying this to the study of religion, Blondel claims that modern philosophy is finally able to discuss the transcendent without absorbing it. Yet even modern philosophy has not become sufficiently aware of its own insufficiency.

Apart from the oversimplification of Blondel's judgment on medieval philosophy and his apparent lack of acquaintance with more ontological trends in modern thought (for instance, Hegel), his position implies that what prevents philosophy from fully grasping the supernatural is not so much the limitation of the experience itself on which philosophy reflects, as the deficiency of reflection with respect to the living experience.

The same attitude seems to lie at the bottom of Blondel's controversial "wager-argument."[21] Here also living action overcomes the abyss between the immanent and the transcendent. In action the supernatural becomes a reality of experience.

What one cannot know nor, above all, understand distinctly, one can always do and practice: that is the use, the eminent reason of action. . . . Its mediation is permanent: it is a perpetual means of internal conversion.[22]

Blondel here opens to the experience of action what he had closed to reflection. But, is the supernatural not as transcendent to practice as it is to thought? Of course, a person may go through the motions of worship, but unless his behavior is at least partially inspired by an initial act of faith (which lies beyond action), it will remain as meaningless as the rote recitation of a religious creed. By itself action never entails conversion. Blondel's attempt to bridge the natural order with the supernatural by means of action, will strike the religious man as a voluntaristic immanentism, and the philosopher as an abdication of reason.

Yet, it is unfair to identify every single ambiguity in Blondel's thought with the error to which it might lead. This was done so often in the past that the importance of his basic ideas has been lost in sterile controversies. A more profitable attitude is exemplified by Duméry who, following Blondel's intuition and methodology, constructed the most significant philosophy of religion of our time.

## NOTES

1. *Lettre sur les exigences de la pensée contemporaine en matière d'apologetique* (Paris, 1962), p. 35. My translation.

2. I shall limit the discussion to *L'action* (1893) and *Lettre sur les exigences de la pensée contemporaine en matière d'apologétique* (1896) in which Blondel's thought comes through much clearer and undistorted by the theological controversies which affected his later work.

3. *L'action* (1893). (Republished by Presses Universitaires de France, 1950), p. 89.

4. *L'action*, p. 91.

5. Gestalt psychology and phenomenology have provided a scientific confirmation of Blondel's insights on this point.

6. *L'action*, p. 107.
7. *L'action*, p. 143.
8. *L'action*, p. 209.
9. *L'action*, p. 321.
10. *L'action*, p. 345.
11. *L'action*, p. 341.
12. *Lettre*, p. 66 (italics ours).
13. *L'action*, p. 321.
14. *L'action*, p. 322.
15. *Lettre*, p. 44.
16. Henry Duméry, *Blondel et la religion* (Paris, 1960), pp. 51-52.
17. *L'action*, pp. 396-397.
18. *Blondel et la religion*, p. 33.
19. Or conceptualism, depending upon whether the emphasis is placed on the phenomena as they appear, or on the rational structures which the mind imposes upon these appearances.
20. *Lettre*, p. 59.
21. The "wager-argument" was first used by Pascal in the following form: You can lose everything by not believing, but you cannot lose anything by believing—therefore, believe. Blondel's version is more an argument for the primacy of action in belief than an argument for belief. In a somewhat simplified fashion it could be summarized as follows: Act as if you believed in order that you may believe.
22. *L'action*, p. 408.

# 6
# Duméry's Reductions of Experience

With Henry Duméry, Kant's tradition comes to an end. What Blondel had initiated, Duméry completed. Instead of *a priori* determining the limits of the religious consciousness, both French philosophers start from that consciousness *as it actually appears*, and then explore its immanent structure—its categories, schemes and specific logic. But while Blondel's method had become more timid after the bold "critique" of his early *L'action*, Duméry refused to be satisfied with a mere *comparison* between the demands of philosophy and the representations of faith, and *subjected* those representations directly to a philosophical critique. In doing so he entirely overcame the Kantian alternative of *either* philosophy *or* faith. Where there was faith philosophy had still full sway. At the same time, philosophy could no longer *dictate* what religion *had to be,* as it had done so often in the past. The problem with philosophy of religion had always been that it was mostly about philosopy and rarely about religion. This is clearly the case in recent times, especially since Kant. But the problem goes back much further to the days when a new branch of metaphysics emerged, later to be called natural theology, which attempted to prove God's existence and to determine his essence *independently of the religious experience within which the very name of God originated.* It was this severance of philosophical God-talk from its religious source which occasioned Pascal's cry: "The God of Abraham, Isaac and Jacob—not the God of the philosophers."

*The New Understanding of Religious Experience*

Several religious thinkers in the last century have tried to lead philosophy of religion away from self-adoration and back to its religious origin. The exodus started with Schleiermacher. Unfortunately, even though the German philosopher had the vision of faith, his romantic lack of appreciation for the intrinsic necessity of symbols prevented him from ever reaching the promised land. Another religious thinker, Søren Kierkegaard, concentrated on deflating the spurious claims of philosophy but spent very little time considering what philosophy *could* do with religion. As a first step in that direction Newman and Blondel attempted to delineate exactly what belonged to the province of faith and what to that of reason. Yet they succeeded merely in establishing a parallelism between reason and religion. If philosophy cannot accomplish more, it fulfills no vital function in the understanding of religion.

Then phenomenology came and opened up entirely new avenues. The phenomenologists set out to discover the meaning of the religious act in the act itself. Rudolf Otto (who was not formally connected with the phenomenological movement but applied its method more successfully than any of its members), Max Scheler, Gerardus Van der Leeuw, Mircea Eliade, all brought reflection to religion without jeopardizing or by-passing the original experience. Some of these results had been anticipated by the American pragmatists William James, Josiah Royce, and William Ernest Hocking. All reflected upon the actual religious experience, instead of attempting to define *a priori* what the religious experience ought to be.

However, the more phenomenology progressed, the more the need for an interpretation of the *roots* of the religious experience was felt. No experience fully reveals its own foundation. The foundation itself, then, can never be phenomenologically described. The case of religion is further complicated by the fact that to the believer religion is not a mere experience. Religion even as it is actually lived does not coincide with the religious experience. To believe means always to accept more than one can understand, see, feel, or in any way experience. Experience in religion is an iceberg that hides more than it reveals. Either religion must remain closed to the light of autonomous reason, or it must be scrutinized by a philosophy that probes beyond experience, that is, beyond what appears. But can a philosophy which is not restricted to the interpretation of experience be prevented from developing into uncontrolled constructivism? The question presents Kant's old predicament in a new form.

Duméry's philosophy offers an affirmative answer. Starting from a phenomenological analysis of the religious experience, it soon moves beyond this experience in order to discover its ontological foundations. By keeping constantly in touch with theological reflection *without ever accepting it at face value*, Duméry avoids losing contact with the believer who finds in theology an authoritative, and, to the extent that he accepts this authority, *intrinsic* interpretation of his experience. This dialogue with theology is all the more justified in that the religious experience itself is not limited to pre-reflective, "lived" religion but includes also the interpretation which religion gives of itself in theology. Faith itself urges on to reflection—*fides quaerens intellectum*. This reflection *on* faith becomes part *of* faith, leading to new religious experiences which in turn will lead to further theological reflection. All too often we think of the religious experience as one thing and theology as another. But, at least in Christianity, theology is part of *every* religious experience. And it has been a serious mistake of philosophy of religion in the past to separate the first "crude" experience from the reflection which continues that experience. This mistake is probably due to the strange but common assumption that the true image of religion is to be found only in its initial, most primitive form.

The philosopher's task is not to invent the experience, but to submit it to the critique of reason. He encounters the idea of God —he is not its author. In that sense, the religious man can never learn anything new from the philosopher. Yet, in another sense, the philosopher makes an important contribution to the *understanding* of the religious experience. A religious experience which excludes philosophical self-understanding would be just as inauthentic as a reflection which is not based upon a previous experience. For religion is not a blind experience; its own impulse urges it on to reflection, and faith necessarily strives for insight. This impulse gives rise to theology, as an attempt to understand the intrinsic coherence of revealed data in the light of the revelation. But the same religious impulse also urges the mind to understand religion, even revealed religion, in the totality of human experience.

This is the task of philosophy. Without philosophy, the religious experience does not fully understand itself. We may conclude, then, that although there is no God of the philosophers, the God of religion is not inaccessible to philosophy.

To the extent that faith belongs to the cognitive order, it must be expressed in intellectual categories over which philosophy has jurisdiction. But in a sense, the entire religious experience is within the jurisdiction of philosophy, since all experience is an object of philosophical reflection. Of course, reflection must not become a substitute for the original experience, but it never will as long as the philosopher keeps in mind the primacy of experience.

This approach is obviously quite different from philosophy's handling of the problem of God in the past. All too often philosophy has simply ignored the reality of faith and, as a result, has said either too little or too much about God. It says too much when it usurps the primacy of the religious experience and substitutes pure reflection in its place. It says too little if, overly fearful of violating the integrity of the religious act, the philosopher restricts himself to developing mere proofs for the existence of God. A contradiction lurks in this exclusive quest for a demonstration of the divine existence, for it implies that God's existence can be known but not his essence, while simultaneously the philosopher endeavors to show that God's essence is identical with his existence.

Duméry proposes that the philosopher devote his energy to a more fruitful enterprise. He should make a critical study of the religious affirmation of God. Faith affirms God on various levels of consciousness: in the intellect, the will, the imagination, the sensibility. The critic's task is to distinguish these levels and to determine the conditions required for the religious affirmation in accordance with each level. He must study the religious act in and through the variety of its expressions. Such a philosophical critique by no means jeopardizes reason's support of faith, nor does it make the proofs for the existence of God superfluous. But it reunites the religious object with the religious affirmation, and refuses to consider the arguments independently of the living affirmation of faith within which they originated. Rather than restricting the role of reason with respect to religion, Duméry's approach gives it a total jurisdiction over the entire field of religious experience. Whatever is experienced falls within the competence of reason. Even the experience of the transcendent is part of the immanent, human reality which reflection has a right to scrutinize and to clarify.

The charge of rationalism which some have raised against this position is ill founded, for as long as reflection stays within the boundaries of the immanent experience, it cannot intrude upon what the religious man considers to be the transcendent origin of this experience. On the contrary, if philosophy does not uphold and exercise its right to reflect critically upon the religious affirmation itself rather than upon some problems which have been carefully excised from this affirmation, one can hardly maintain that it fulfills its task, namely, to clarify the human experience in its totality.

In claiming this right, philosophy merely returns to its origin. Ancient philosophy was well aware of its religious roots and made no attempt to hide or ignore them, as philosophy did later. It is a well-known fact that Western philosophy originated in a reflection upon the religious cosmologies of the Near East. Less known, perhaps, is that the umbilical cord with the living religious experience was maintained for many centuries after the origin of philosophy. For Socrates and Plato, whom we generally regard as the initiators of purely autonomous thinking, philosophy remained religious in form (the myth) and in content. In fact, the mystical trend of Plato's philosophy became the very heart of Plotinus's thought.

In the Middle Ages the relation between philosophy and religion was drastically altered. Revelation became the proper object of the science of theology as such. As a result, except for a few isolated attempts,[1] revealed religion ceased to be an object of philosophical inquiry. The study of revealed religion was not to be taken up again until after Kant. And not until the contemporary phenomenological movement was it *generally* accepted that philosophy might have something positive to say about the entire realm of revealed religion. Even so, phenomenology has remained primarily descriptive. Duméry, however, wants to restore philosophy to its full critical right. The task of philosophy is not merely to describe and analyze but also to evaluate critically on all levels of consciousness, the formation and structure of religious symbols, including the ones which the religious man considers to be strictly revealed.

As we saw earlier, this strictly rational approach is not rationalistic, provided the philosopher does not mistake critical work for actual religion and keeps his reflection subordinate to the living experience. Yet the question may be raised whether it is still adequately distinguished from theology. Duméry answers that the difference between the two disciplines is not one of content but of method. Theology reflects upon the content of faith and so does the philosophy of religion. But whereas the former reflects upon this content from an attitude of faith, the latter may never make its reflection intrinsically dependent upon the acceptance of the content of *faith*. The philosopher accepts the religious affirmation only as a *content of consciousness* without committing himself to the transcendent reality which it affirms. His method is entirely autonomous, not in the sense that it is independent of religious faith, but in the sense that it does not share the basic commitment of that faith. The theologian, on the contrary, is fully committed: he accepts the authority of sacred writings and of the religious community whose beliefs the Scriptures systematize. For the philosopher, this authority is part of a total experience, but it is not singled out as a determining motive moving him to unconditional adherence. It is precisely the acceptance of a transcendent authority *within the reflection itself* that makes theological conclusions essentially different from philosophical ones.

The philosophical *epoche* does not imply, however, that philosophy and theology have only the material content of their object in common. Theology constantly borrows from philosophy, both in content and in method, to reach its own conclusions. Similarly, philosophy reflects upon the *total* religious experience, which includes theology. For all its autonomy, philosophy of religion would have little to reflect upon were it not for the existence of theology. Rather than avoiding the theologian, the philosopher of religion must try to situate what the theologian is doing within the *total* experience of life. In that function he provides, perhaps unwittingly, a link between philosophy and theology.

The language of the theologian is disconcerting for philosophers only insofar as they are unable to discover what the theologian wants to say in what he actually says. As for himself, the theologian knows it very well where his practice and that of the believer is concerned. But he does not always know it critically, and he need not know it that way. The philosopher of religion understands his enterprise. Without substituting anything for the religious sense held by the theologian, he still can elucidate it in a methodical and critical way.[2]

In defining the method of philosophy of religion Duméry was strongly influenced by Maurice Blondel. Ever since his dissertation on *L'action* Duméry has retained contact with the French philosopher's thought. Today he is probably his most perceptive interpreter. Of particular influence on his own thought was Blondel's view on the relation between philosophy and living experience. The reality of living experience is accessible only to action. Philosophy does not deal with it. Its task is solely to discover logical coherence, and particularly the inner system of determinations of action. No logical structure can ever replace the primary experience of the real. But at the same time this limitation allows philosophy to reflect upon all of reality without ever illegitimately intruding into the proper domain of action. Thus the philosopher can with all due respect for the transcendent reality of revealed religion study it as a self-contained system of thought. For he never discusses this reality as such but only the logical structure in which it is presented.

Any philosophy which does not by its very nature exclude the possibility or the cognition of man's relation to the transcendent must consider the study of the religious phenomenon a logical necessity. Blondel explains this necessity as the need to overcome the discrepancy between the infinite impulse of action and its limited achievements.

All attempts to bring human action to completion fail, and yet human action cannot but strive to complete itself and to suffice to itself. It must but it cannot. The feeling of impotence as well as that of the need for an infinite consummation remain incurable.[3]

This discrepancy makes the question of a transcendent completion logically inevitable. Now, the believer claims that such a completion is achieved in revealed religion. In his search for coherence in the system of determination of action the philosopher cannot simply dismiss this claim. According to Blondel, he must consider it at least as a logically necessary hypothesis.

Yet Duméry's philosophy is more than a critique of noetic structures. It is above all an attempt to discover the foundation of the religious experience. No experience, least of all the religious one, reveals its own foundation. A mere critique of the structures of experience and expression cannot claim to be an exhaustive reflection upon the religious reality. If philosophy is to remain adequate to its task of total reflection it must probe beyond the actual phenomenon. Yet here we meet the particular difficulty of all religion: the ultimate reality intended by the religious act must because of its transcendent nature remain unknown. Can philosophy confronted with the transcendent do more than abstain and abdicate? The point is important for the religious attitude itself, since faith loses all rational justification if its basis is withdrawn from rational scrutiny. It becomes mere instinct, feeling or whatever one may call a state of consciousness in which truth is allowed no part. Having embraced the position of negative theology on the mind's ultimate inability to know God and at the same time advocating its full accessibility to the rational, Duméry must have felt strongly the impact of this difficulty. Once again, the principles of Blondel's *L'action* showed him the way out of his predicament.

Underneath all human activity he detects the mind's positive surge toward an ultimate principle that is beyond all determination. This surge appears in all forms of human activity. Cognition, desire, feeling, all manifest a constant striving towards absolute unity. The search for an ultimate principle is precisely what, according to Duméry, Plotinus's philosophy of the One attempts to express. The One is identical with the mind as the principle which enables the mind to posit itself. Yet, the mind cannot be said to *be* the One since it labors under a subject-object opposition. The One is present in the mind's striving, not in its realization. Only a total adherence to this absolute unity will allow the mind to terminate its striving.

Plotinus's impact on Duméry's thought is so strong that one

might call him a neo-Platonist, were it not for the even more considerable influence of Husserl on his philosophy. From him Duméry borrows the technical equipment for his *itinerarium mentis ad Deum*: Plotinus's stages of the mind's conversion to the One are presented as the reductions of Husserl's phenomenology.

In the first, so-called *eidetic* reduction, the mind eliminates all factual, contingent elements from the phenomena of consciousness in order to grasp their universal essences. A second reduction, called *transcendental* or *phenomenological*, "brackets" all reference to existential reality in order to concentrate exclusively on the phenomena in their relatedness to the transcendental subject.

> The phenomenological reduction is the awareness of the subordination of the essences to the act which mediates itself through them, which expresses itself in them and reconquers itself upon them.[4]

A third, *egological* reduction views the phenomena of consciousness as not merely related to, but also *produced* by the transcendental subject. The study of the constitution of mental phenomena thus becomes a study of the transcendental ego.

Duméry considers these three reductions indispensable in any philosophical analysis. But since, at Husserl's own admission, no ultimate absolute can be reached through them, Duméry feels the need for a fourth, *henological* reduction, grounding the transcendental ego itself in the absolute One. Without this final reduction the mind's striving for unity is not sufficiently founded. But before discussing this innovation, it may be appropriate to bring out some of the implications of the phenomenological method as Duméry understands it.

For Duméry as for Husserl, consciousness and the conscious object constitute one ideal unit of meaning. Neither an independent world of objects nor an independent consciousness confronting the world of objects makes sense to Duméry. Things first acquire meaning and become objects under the intentional gaze of consciousness. "There are only intentional objects, because there is no consciousness but objectifying consciousness."[5] Thus, it is Husserl's theory of the transcendental reduction that provides the epistemological foundation for Duméry's theory of the creative self.


## Autonomy and the Act-Law

No epoch has been more aware of man's freedom than our own, and no philosophy has given a stronger expression to this awareness than existentialism. To be free, for the existentialist, means more than to choose among given possibilities—it means to create possibilities. Authentic freedom, then, is compatible with any fixed and predetermined order of values and ideas. For the same reason, Sartre asserts, freedom also excludes God, for if God exists man can no longer create his values—at most he can accept and ratify pre-created values. But such an acceptance is an escape from the task of authentic freedom: it leaves man none but a negative creativity of evil. "A God who would be the arsenal of eternal truths, who would have made all the good and the true, would not have left us anything to do but evil which is the opposite of being."[6]

In Sartre's philosophy freedom has no ulterior foundation. The free act reposes entirely upon itself. As soon as it accepts anything as *given*, freedom loses its authenticity. Of course, Sartre does not deny the opaque reality of the world within which freedom operates. But this reality is a resistance—to be fought rather than accepted. Nor does authentic freedom ever become trapped in its own creations. As soon as a value has been conquered, it becomes part of an objective, thing-like universe and must be rejected if freedom is to remain free. Sartre's freedom, therefore, is bound to remain entirely negative: it destroys but does not construct. And since this negative freedom has no further foundation, it cannot be but a useless passion.

Duméry agrees with Sartre that a preexisting realm of truth and value would indeed restrict man's intellectual and moral autonomy and would, therefore, be destructive of authentic freedom. But he denies that the existence of God implies a pre-established order of values. In the neo-Platonic tradition which Duméry follows, God is without any determinations. All values, intellectual and moral, are created by the finite spirit. Yet the creative impulse itself can be explained only by means of a transcendent and trans-ordinal principle. "The creative freedom which for Sartre and Polin is possible only in the refusal of God, is declared to be impossible without God by Plotinus."[7]

God creates no values, but he is at the origin of man's value-creating *activity*. Dependence, then, is the source of man's autonomy, and createdness the root of his creativity. Creativity requires an energy beyond all determinations: the finite spirit creates all determinations but God creates his determining activity. No conflicts can arise because the determinate order and the trans-ordinal belong to different levels. Rather than imposing values upon me, God has made me able to create them myself.

Nevertheless, Duméry feels that theism can profit a good deal by the criticism of existentialist theism. It forces the believer to face his responsibility in this world, instead of leaving to God what is essentially man's own task. Sartre, then, may lead the way back to a more authentic affirmation of God such as was made by Plotinus for whom God is active in his creation without ever imposing any finite determination.

Important practical conclusions follow from this insight. One of them is that any form of faith which impairs freedom of conscience necessarily conflicts with the nature of true religion. Religious intolerance always results from an erroneous notion of God. It conceives him as an object, the supreme object containing all the values and ideas which the mind must obediently accept. Since truth in this attitude is to be received rather than created, there can be no truth in the non-believer except where he agrees with the believer. At most the believing community can "tolerate" his error and this only on condition that intolerance would be even more detrimental to a universal acceptance of the truth. But in a homogeneous religious society the tendency will always be to make the non-believer conform as much as possible and to force him to accept a truth which is by its very nature monolithic.

Such an attitude jeopardizes God's transcendence. God is not the *locus veritatis*—his truth is above human knowledge, just as his goodness is above human striving. As long as the believer fails to see this fact he will be intolerant of others and cheat his way out of his responsibilities. For if God is the ultimate answer to all questions, then the acceptance of his revelation guarantees the believer the full possession of all religious and moral truth. He then is dispensed from the painful search for truth and can confidently consider his view on life superior to that of the non-believer.

The intolerant believer always identifies his religious experience with an objectivistic value theory. But far from being implied in the religious experience, objectivism can only diminish its authenticity. Few ideas have proved more harmful to religion than the idea that the religious man *possesses* the truth. To be sure, there is a religious truth communicated through revelation and guaranteed by divine authority. But this truth is of a very peculiar sort: it is a *way of salvation*. It presupposes the existence of values, and it provides man with norms to integrate these values. Even these norms have been expressed in a human way, which again accounts for greater or lesser perfection.

*Absolutely* true is only the believer's relation to God and God's own assistance (including the one of his Word) to preserve this attachment. Such a relation by no means implies an adhesion to a number of values and ideas, preexisting in the divine essence. "The true and the good are not pre-posited in God (which in the ultimate analysis makes no sense); they are created, posited and invented by man within his relationship to God."[8]

Consciousness alone constitutes meaning and value. Yet, this does not imply that consciousness can create meaning at random, independent of rule and law. The meaning-giving *ego* is not the empirical self but the transcendental *ego*, which constitutes both the self and the world. Duméry calls this more profound, creative ego *act-law*. It is an *act* because it creates, produces, and regulates. The ego acts autonomously but not independently: it receives its active impulse from the One which is above all determinations. This One is the object of the fourth, *henological* reduction. It reveals the ultimate, unconditioned condition of the ego. In its constituting activity the self determines the indeterminate energy of the One. The self, then, is not an original creative principle as the One is: it is an act which is *pre-ordained* to determine being according to its immanent necessity, and which therefore rightly may be called *law*. The determination of all being is a necessary condition (Hegel would say a *mediation*) for the self's conversion to the One.

Still, the question remains: How can the self be a law to itself without being arbitrary? Duméry's answer is clear. In the creation of meaning and value *the self expresses its essential relation to the One*. Man's creative activity reveals his thrust toward the One. This henological direction of the self's creativity excludes all arbitrariness. Undoubtedly, man may jeopardize the mediating function of his activity by overemphasizing some values to the detriment of all others. Yet, this error does not result from the creative act itself, but from man's failure to recognize its relativity, that is, its relatedness to the One, which alone is absolute.

It is important to keep in mind that the ego's creativity does not follow from the awareness of the self, but that it precedes it as its necessary condition. Man constitutes meanings and values before he experiences himself as a constituting ego. Even this awareness does not reveal the act-law directly, but only its expressions. The task of philosophy consists in discovering the ego's original, intentional impulse underneath these conscious expressions and in understanding constituted ideas and values as objectifications of more fundamental attitudes. Philosophy thus brings into reflective focus the most basic activity of the mind from which the empirical self originates.

The distinction between act-law and empirical consciousness is essential. It allows Duméry to eliminate several false problems. One such problem is the opposition between freedom and determinism. As long as consciousness remains restricted to what is empirically accessible, freedom is simply an unexplainable exception in a deterministic world. As the positive sciences (one of which is psychology) draw ever narrower circles around its little enclave, the suspicion grows that some day scientific predictability will cover a field which a lack of knowledge alone still withholds from complete determinism. In Duméry's view, however, scientific determination itself originates in the creative spontaneity of the ego. Instead of suppressing freedom, determinism presupposes it. For rather than merely ratifying a preexisting objective necessity, freedom, for Duméry, is the subjective but necessary source of all objective determinism.

Of course, the freedom which produces necessity is by no means arbitrary; it cannot even be identified with the traditional "freedom of indifference." It surpasses the psychological experience of deliberation as well as the unclassifiable phenomena that remain after the scientist has finished his work. If the pre-scientific concept of unlimited freedom is too simplistic, the positive notion of an all-comprehensive preexisting determinism is even more so.

Psychological consciousness knows only those causalities which could originate from its own choices, or fragments of causality of which it does not know the ins and outs, or, finally, the not-further-justifiable shock of factualness. Never except by illegitimate extension or generalisation is it aware of a necessity at once intelligible and impelling. Similarly, the scientist discovers phenomenal connections, experimental concatenations. He supposes determinism wherever nature does not respond *no* to his question, wherever the precision of his calculation allows him to tie together phenomena which must be integrated into an operative whole. But never does he find himself confronted by a fully constituted causalism. Order supposes an organizer. The experimental structures are those of the laboratory, that is, of man and his instruments, not of nature.[9]

If determinism cannot exist without freedom, neither can freedom exist without determination. Freedom and arbitrariness exclude each other. The act-law is essentially *order*, and order means determination, but the determination is the self's determination, the order is the self's order, not one imposed from without. Even to place God under the denominator of *being* would make man dependent upon God in the order of determination, and would be incompatible with the autonomy of the *act-law*. Duméry therefore rejects the traditional notion of participation. Being and the source of being cannot share in the same being. As to the principle of determination, Plotinus's *intelligible*, it *proceeds* from the One, but does not participate in the One. Henology and participation exclude each other. "One must choose between these two possibilities. The advantage of the henology is that it simultaneously guarantees the radical productivity of the One and the creativity of the intelligible, the One as 'source-principle' and the intelligible as self-position."[10]

## Negative Theology and Revelation

This radical status of the self's creative autonomy raises several questions. The first one is: If God is above all categories, how can we know about him? Any form of "natural theology" seems to be excluded. Even to prove God's "existence" is not possible—much less to discover his attributes. Duméry is not deterred by this negative conclusion, for it forces him to lay all the more stress upon the notion of *revelation*. Man cannot but make the movement toward God, yet he cannot *know* God unless God reveals himself.

Because he cannot himself speak our language, all speculative revelation becomes impossible. That is why the Bible declares fruitless all human wisdom which claims to teach us *in toto* or in part what God is.[11]

One may wonder, however, whether Duméry's radically negative theology has not eliminated even the possibility of a revelation. Some critics think that he has removed God so far from man as to make any subsequent contact impossible. Duméry answers this objection in the second edition of *La foi n'est pas un cri*. He admits that God is silent insofar as he transcends all determinations of language. But God can reveal himself insofar as he is the source of our speaking. If the henological reduction can be made, a dialogue with God is possible. Duméry may "reduce" a substantial part of what the ordinary believer considers to be essential to the notion of revelation. But he stresses just as strongly the possibility of, and the need for, a revelation.

God is beyond our grasp, our categories, but he appears through them. He is the high point of our aims, he is their soul. Nevertheless, we must increasingly purify our ideas and our schemas. For instance, he cannot be called *personal*—personal as we are; but he is more. It is possible, it is normal to address ourselves to him as to a person, provided we preserve the mystery.[12]

Definitely eliminated in Duméry's thought is a revelation of God through nature. Nature may help man find his way to God, but it can never teach him anything *about* God. Nature has no voice of its own—all revelation is essentially human, for man alone can give meaning and expression. So, if God is to speak at all, he must do it through man. Man alone is the image of God.

But this brings us to a second question. If man alone has the power of speech and if God is above all human categories, how can any revelation be said to be *God's* Word? Revelation seems to be an expression of man, in both its content and its form. In constituting the sacred, the human subject creates mediating schemas and categories in order to attain the Absolute. As expressions of a human experience, these schemas and categories are obviously human. So, then, what entitles the religious man to read God's Word in them? If they are merely intermediate stages in the mind's ascent to the One, they are at best relative expressions. How, then, can the believer ascribe a permanent, absolute meaning to the words of revelation? If the One is above all intelligible determination, why should the New Testament be anything more than the relation to the Absolute of one particular cultural group expressed in accordance with its specific needs and aspirations? Duméry would admit the relativity of all religious language, including that of the New Testament. Every language bears the imprint of the civilization which it expresses, and that civilization is, by its very nature, relative. But he would deny that this relativity eliminates the absolute element. The transcendent nature of God does not exclude an objective revelation—nor does the subjective acceptance and expression of this revelation, the so-called projection, eliminate its objective character.

Consciousness does not project anything *upon* the object, it does not cover it with something that does not belong to it. I use the term projective consciousness as opposed to reflective consciousness. I mean that consciousness itself is spontaneously projective: it projects, not something of itself upon something other than itself, but the meanings which it intends on a diversity of expressive levels. Its act is intentional: it is directed toward the object and attains it; but it cannot intend it without expressing it at the same time in a spectrum of various representations.[13]

Subjective structures do not change the object: they are the indispensable means by which the subject attains objective essences on various levels of consciousness. They are the prism in which the object itself is refracted. That the New Testament projects the religious consciousness of a particular community, by no means implies that it has deformed the objective character of the *fact* Jesus. Indeed, without such a projection there would be no religious history. For what transforms these particular facts into *religious* facts if not their mode of acceptance? For meaning, history must depend on meaning-giving subjects. This is particularly true in the case of sacred history. The events of Jesus' life can have a religious meaning only to a religious subject. To *understand* the religious meaning of Christ, it is not sufficient to register the historical facts of his existence.

The religious reality objectively contains the meaning which the believer recognizes in it; yet, this meaning is perceived only when the believer discerns this reality as religious. In technical terms: the religious object exists, but we still must "constitute" it as religious.[14]

The most essential characteristic of the religious object is that it must be received in a religious way, that is, that it must be *given* a religious meaning.

Far from being a deviation from the original message, the interpretation of faith is a necessary factor for the correct transmission of this message. For the message itself refers to faith and this cannot be transmitted by a merely factual report. It requires a personal commitment on the part of the reporter. If the evangelists had not told their story in a spirit of faith, their writings would have been no more "sacred" than the brief reports on Christ in Tacitus and Pliny. Historical reliability requires that the events be rendered as truthfully as possible—*not* that the narrator abstain from all religious interpretation, for this interpretation is an essential part of the events *insofar as they are religious.*

The religious interpretation also justifies the selection which the sacred narrators apply to their historical material, and which must appear quite arbitrary to the non-believer. Even many believers who imagine that it suffices to "get the facts" in order to have faith are shocked by this selection and prefer to ignore it. But every history requires *some* selection, and since a "religious fact" can be recognized only in a religious vision, a selection of facts on the basis of their religious acceptance becomes imperative. Duméry's position supports the conclusion of contemporary biblical scholarship, that the sacred writers found their inspiration within a religious tradition and must be read in that tradition. The tradition is the faith of the witnessing community which is able to bestow the religious meaning upon historical events.

Yet the necessity of a subjective acceptance in faith, of a tradition, does not reduce religion to a merely subjective experience.[15] Christianity has always strongly emphasized the historical character of its foundation. The object of Christian faith can be seen only through the eyes of faith, yet faith itself requires that its object be *historical*. The religious vision of faith is empty without the historical facts which it illuminates. An attack upon the historicity of the basic events of Christianity, Jesus' death and resurrection, is, therefore, an attack upon Christianity itself. No doubt, faith in the resurrection goes far beyond the historical apparitions and the discovery of the empty tomb: it demands that death and resurrection be accepted as essential stages of the revelation of the Son of God and of the redemption of man. Yet the act of faith itself needs the foundation of historical facts. Only a dialectic of seeing and believing could ever lead to the pentecostal experience.

The apparitions of Christ are proofs, because they do not merely present the risen Christ to seers, but to seers who are also believers and whose belief brings them to the proper perspective, to an order of truth in which it would be contradictory to claim that Jesus is the Christ, the blessed of God, without having broken the bonds of death.[16]

The apostles believed because they saw and they saw because they believed.

Another point that must be emphasized against any subjectivist interpretation of man's theophanic activity in Christianity is that the original and most basic meaning of Jesus' acts was given by Jesus himself. This meaning was reconstituted and developed by the primitive Christian community. The result was transmitted to later generations who, in turn, reconstituted these objective data into religious experiences. Since the meaning-giving activity is obviously conditioned by the personal characteristics and the cultural level of the interpreters, the religious interpretation of "the Jesus event" varies from age to age. Yet, all these variations do not basically deviate from the original meaning given by Jesus himself. Against the position of *form-criticism* Duméry maintains that the collective consciousness may enrich an idea, but that the idea itself can originate only in a personal consciousness. What the Christian community sees in Christ was, at least implicitly, immanent in Jesus' experience. To recognize Jesus as the Lord is an act of faith that no historical "facts" can "substantiate." Still, the Christian's belief cannot be without objective support. For why is it that the believer's faith centers exclusively upon Christ, while he rejects all other "theophanies"? Whatever the basis of such a religious discrimination may be, it cannot be purely subjective. As Duméry remarks:

The religious consciousness deifies only those beings that display for its eyes a presence indicating divine authority. Every theophany is a value judgment, the value of which is proportionate to the spiritual requirements of him who formulates it. How could we deny that in the case of Christ and his disciples the theophanic judgment passed on Jesus was inspired by his own attitude through which it attained a particularly pure conception of the nature of God.[17]

Some objective religious meaning must obviously be transmitted. Since such a meaning is not immanent in the historical events as such, it must be placed in them by a religious interpretation of the events. In Christianity, this interpretation started with Jesus and his first disciples. Yet, the believer may wonder, is Jesus not more than a genial interpreter of man's striving toward transcendence? Is he not, more than a mere occasion of faith for the believer, a transcendent savior? Has the significance not shifted entirely from the event to the interpretation and the distinction between myth and history all but disappeared?

A revelation in the believer's understanding of the term is given in a specific form and invites a specific response. In Duméry one feels that both the appeal and the response are in the final analysis wholly immanent. To be sure, every concrete religious expression is contingent and human. But that does not justify an absolute distinction between impulse and expression. Either both must be transcendent (as well as immanent) or neither one is. Duméry interprets all determinations of the religious act—including such basic ones as revelation and salvation—as structures created by the mind's own impulse toward a mystery which is neither determined nor determining. He thus separates the religious expression from the religious intentionality which inspired it. Only the religious impulse originates in the transcendent ground of consciousness; the concrete determinations in which this impulse expresses itself are entirely immanent and carry no transcendent meaning of their own. They are posited, rather than received, by the mind. Such a position reveals in spite of strong assertions to the contrary, a somewhat disincarnated concept of religion. It would also seem to necessitate the demythologization which Duméry persistently rejects. But above all, such a conception ultimately jeopardizes the notion of a revelation as positive communication from the transcendent. The eternal object of the revelation, as well as its historical manifestations, is deprived of the very determinations which for the faithful make the religious experience more than an immanent striving of the mind toward the ground of all being. The Christian dogma of the Holy Trinity, for example, is no more than an epistemic construction, determined by a cultural tradition, which the mind *uses* in its surge toward an inaccessible transcendent.

## NOTES

1. The most brilliant of which was Spinoza's.
2. *La tentation de faire du bien* (Paris, 1956), p. 158.
3. *L'action*, p. 321.
4. *Critique et religion* (Paris, 1957), p. 147.
5. *Philosophie de la religion* (Paris, 1957), I, p. 21.
6. *Foi et interrogation* (Paris, 1953), p. 33.
7. *La tentation de faire du bien* (Paris, 1956), p. 153.
8. *Ibid.*, p. 57.
9. *Philosophie de la religion*, I, p. 60.
10. *Henk Van Luyk, La philosophie du fait chrétien* (Paris, 1965), p. 78.
11. *La foi n'est pas un cri* (Paris, 1959), p. 216.
12. *Ibid.*, p. 225.
13. *Ibid.*, pp. 224-45.
14. *Ibid.*, p. 258.
15. *Loc. cit.*
16. *Ibid.*, p. 83.
17. *Ibid.*, p. 74.

# Part III
# The Justification of Religious Faith

# 7
# The Cosmological Argument

The core of Kant's critique of the arguments for the existence of God is that the phenomenal world, sole object of human cognition, can never provide information about what by definition transcends it. The transcendent ideal of human knowledge may be used as a regulative idea; it can never be given a scientifically reliable content. Those principles have not remained unchallenged. According to a number of post-Kantian philosophers starting with Fichte, human knowledge reaches well beyond the phenomenal. Yet such a widening of the scope of philosophy still does not answer the question how a specific positive content can be given to the notion of transcendence. Even if human knowledge reaches beyond the phenomenal, are we justified in equating a transcendent limit or horizon with the religious idea of God? In this and the following two chapters, I shall consider how Kant's critique affected the arguments' subsequent existence. Did they ever recover? Have they been given new strength? Completeness is, of course, the last quality these considerations could claim. The renewed interest in natural theology in recent years has spawned an almost endless series of monographs and essays on the subject. One conclusion emerges fairly consistently. Kant's critique has not been "refuted," even though much of it has to be qualified. Yet this negative conclusion has led to a new awareness of what the so-called arguments really are, and what they were at their origin: an attempt to translate into logical form what the religious attitude is in practice.

*Causality and Contingency*

A proper evaluation of attempts to revive what Kant referred to as the "cosmological argument" requires separate consideration

131

of the original two proofs on causality and contingency that entered into it. In addition, we must also consider St. Thomas' "fourth way," based on the degrees of perfection by means of which some moderns have tried to strengthen the other two. Yet the requirement of a first cause remains the central part of the cosmological argument. In the original version the necessity was deduced from the existence of efficient causality in the world. Since all known causes have been caused by others and none by itself, an uncaused cause outside the chain is needed to support the causal process. An infinite regress of caused causes, though not contradictory, fails to account for the causal activity *as such*. The term "first cause" then refers to an ontological rather than a chronological primacy. Not the point of origin of the causal process requires a transcendent explanation, but its very existence at any given time.

The argument received its first major blow when Hume questioned the objective validity of the principle of causality itself. Being derived from three different impressions—contiguity, temporal priority and constant conjunction—the idea of causality remains restricted by the quality of those impressions. The additional feeling of necessity evoked by the repeated and constant connection of the two phenomena in the described order must remain purely subjective, since it has no basis in sensation. Having thus deprived the principle of its objective certitude, Hume further undermined its applicability beyond the realm of observation by his elementarist axiom: What can be conceived separately may exist independently. If "effects" of known causes may be conceived separately, *a fortiori* can we conceive as independently existing that which we have never directly experienced to be subject to causal efficacy.

Hume's sweeping critique was attacked on several counts. Even what appeared to be his strongest assertion, the denial of the existence of an "impression" of causality, was challenged by experiments ascertaining the direct perception of causality.[1] Yet sense perception was never the crucial issue, since to have any probative value at all, the principle of causality must be conceived as essentially a rational principle. To be sure, if, as Hume claims, "causes and effects are discoverable not by reason but by experience"[2] no causal efficacy can be established beyond the range of direct sense perception. But no evidence supports this dogmatic empiricism. Hume's elementarism (whatever can be conceived separately can exist independently) must be challenged as equally dogmatic.

Yet to refute Hume is one thing. To salvage the use of the principle of causality in the cosmological argument is another. Even without empiricist and elementarist prejudice the extension beyond the physical universe of a notion conceived to describe phenomena within this universe, remains problematic. Kant who had risen vigorously to the defense of a principle which he deemed indispensable for the proper pursuit of scientific investigation, nevertheless concluded that we must abstain from using it beyond the phenomenal realm; "The principle of causality has no meaning and no criterion for its application save only in the sensible world. But in the cosmological proof it is precisely in order to enable us to advance beyond the sensible world that it is employed."[3] How appropriate is the term "first cause" within the (irrefutable) hypothesis of a universe without beginning?[4] Finally, more and more philosophers have started questioning whether the concept of cause ought not to be abandoned altogether because of our inability to give it a precise and useful meaning.[5] Others, perceiving that even those who reject the notion as useless continue to employ it, prefer to redefine it. One of the more interesting attempts may be found in a recent study of the cosmological argument. Professor Reichenbach defines as cause the conditions individually necessary and jointly sufficient for the occurrence of a particular "effect."[6] Without the known presence of all the conditions the author claims, the effect is not truly intelligible. Though we may not be able to understand all the conditions adequately, the very possibility of scientific investigation requires nevertheless their actual fulfillment. Now, the argument continues, the conditions are not fulfilled unless we also include the existence of an ultimate condition, a reality on which all other beings depend without being dependent on them. Without it the universe as a whole remains unintelligible and, consequently, also the final explanation of each phenomenon in it is lacking. But the ultimate condition cannot be found within the series. Even if conditioned beings would constitute a closed chain of conditioners which are themselves conditioned, they still

would fail to make their functioning intelligible. Only a being unconditioned in every respect would suffice in this task.[7] Not to
require, then, the existence of a transcendent cause or extra-serial
ultimate condition conflicts with the basic presupposition in the
scientist's search for the explanation of the phenomenal object of
his investigation.

Two questions may be raised about this usage of the rein-
terpreted causal principle in the cosmological argument. 1) How
intelligible must the universe be to allow practical action and scientific investigation? 2) How much intelligibility does the acceptance
of a *transcendent* unconditioned condition add? The first question
was raised by Bertrand Russell in his famous B.B.C. debate with
Father Copleston: "When is an explanation adequate?" If it must
be exhaustive, as Fr. Copleston demanded, no explanation will
ever be adequate.[8] The kind of complete intellectual satisfaction
which we so easily attain in the order of mathematics is excluded
in the order of causality. As C.D. Broad noted: "It is quite certain
that no explanation in terms of ordinary causation is capable of
giving this kind of satisfaction to the intellect. For no causal law
has any trace of self-evidence."[9] Would our chances of gaining this
satisfaction considerably increase by postulating a "first" cause? I
think not. The proponents themselves never pretended to have a
clear insight into the mode of the transcendent cause's condition-
ing. They merely insist that it must be present. But if we do not
know how the ultimate condition conditions, how can we claim
that it alone makes the process of knowledge ultimately intelligible? I cannot conceive of it in any other way than as cause or as
necessary being. It may be difficult to conceive of events taking
place in our universe without some sort of causal connection with
other events. But applied beyond the physical universe, the catego-
ry seems to lose its foothold altogether.[10] At this point I do not
want to dispute the need for an unconditioned condition in the case
of the universe as a whole. But since we are at a total loss about its
function, I fail to see how any intelligibility could be gained by
conceiving it one way or another. Specifically with respect to the
second question, I detect no gain in intelligibility from conceiving
the ultimate condition transcendent rather than immanent. Without recurring to an infinite regress of conditioned conditions, one

may conceive of the unconditioned as existing within the series of conditions. Yet to investigate those possibilities we must abandon the notion of efficient causality altogether. For at least in its ordinary conception, causality with respect to the whole already presupposes a transcendent relation.

In this respect the concept of sufficient reason presents a distinct advantage over that of causality. For a cause, as Kant pointed out in his critique of Leibniz's metaphysics, must always remain extrinsic to its effect (and since it also surpasses that effect, we would automatically have to call it transcendent), while a sufficient reason may well be intrinsic to the being whose existence it justifies. In demanding a sufficient reason for the existence of the universe at least one does not prejudge the case. Within the context of the argument we may safely quote sufficient reason with the intrinsic necessity which Saint Thomas so judiciously distinguished from causality. Thomas had followed Avicenna in defining as necessary that whose non-existence involves a logical contradiction—a definition which seventeenth century philosophers would adopt again. But in the *Summa Theologiae*, Thomas apparently felt the need for a more verifiable criterion and defined as necessary a being not subject to generation and corruption. Scholastic versions of the argument after Aquinas take it mostly for granted that contingency (i.e., the opposite of necessity, by Thomas named "possibility") is inherently connected with a being's beginning and ceasing to exist. To achieve the transition from non-existence to existence, a temporal being must depend on another one, and such dependence is clearly incompatible with intrinsic necessity.

Yet the equation of contingency with limited existence presupposes that each being is ontologically distinct from all others. I am by no means sure that this is the only acceptable view. Significantly enough, Thomas himself did not regard beginning and end as adequate criteria of contingency. In defining as necessary a being that is not *generated* and cannot be *corrupted* he deliberately left room for necessary beings with a beginning and the possibility of an end, such as heavenly bodies and human souls.[11] Yet my purpose here is not to defend St. Thomas' position, for in his view necessary beings that have a beginning are still dependent for their existence upon a transcendent being "having of itself its own necessity and not receiving it from another."[12] Moreover, at this point, St. Thomas returns the argument to causality: whatever can be and not be must have a transcendent cause, otherwise there would have been a "time" when nothing existed. After the preceding discussion of the difficulties inherent in the transcendent usage of the concept of causality, we should be reluctant to follow the argument back onto that trail and prefer to consider generation and corruption merely as symptoms of contingency, not as indicators of the need of a first cause.

Unfortunately, they provide no more certitude of contingency than the beginning or, for that matter, any other aspect of phenomenal being would provide. To be sure, if a being begins to exist and, even more clearly, if it is generated, it cannot possess its total *raison d'être* in itself, since it cannot bring itself into being. But this need not result in the existence of a *transcendent* necessity. A temporal being might still come into existence as a necessary link in a process developing by *immanent* necessity, as some evolutionary or process philosophers claim. Until the latter view has been refuted, the possibility of a temporal being receiving its necessity from the process itself of which it constitutes an intrinsic part, cannot be excluded. Even before the evolutionary systems appeared, Spinoza considered the finite to be a "mode" of the infinite substance from which it is distinct but not detached. One of the few modern scholastics who paid attention to this in his discussion of the argument of contingency was forced to concede: "All one can conclude from the fact that a being ceases to exists is that there is a certain distinction between that being and the being which exists through its own essence. But such a distinction is not necessarily identical with the one between a creature and a transcendent Creator. The particular being may well be a mere mode of the being which exists through its own essence. In that case it becomes meaningless to say that it does not have in itself the reason for its existence.[13]

The objection which Reichenbach raises against the infinite series, namely that it lacks at least one more condition for the existence of the series, remains powerless against a process which *creates* its conditions as it develops. However, a process without a transcendent principle must be conceived as beginningless. Otherwise it would have brought itself into existence. This imposes severe restrictions on the notion, all the more so since scientists show but little sympathy for a universe without beginning.

Finally, we must raise the basic question whether the universe needs a sufficient reason. Thus far we have assumed that the contingent requires the necessary, provided one can ever identify a being as contingent. But our lack of success in achieving the latter task raises the suspicion that the distinction itself may be fictitious. Is the search for a "sufficient reason" not a futile enterprise? Granted, certain things do not strike us as self-explanatory and many situations may appear purely gratuitous or even absurd. But is that in itself a sufficient basis for not considering them as ultimate? It would be, of course, if the very intelligibility of the universe required for scientific research and practical action were to be jeopardized without an ultimate "reason." But there is no evidence that such is the case, for the intelligibility of the universe needed for those purposes requires no more than a certain order and regularity *within* the world. Even those who consider the world "absurd" (i.e., totally gratuitous, without even the possibility of a rational foundation) are able to operate in it.

The question, then, boils down to this: Does an irrational ultimate conflict with what we know about this world? Or is it at least less acceptable than a rational one. John Hick who discusses this question concedes: "As *de facto* ultimate, God and the physical universe enjoy an equal status."[14] One provides a de jure terminus to the explanatory process, the other merely a de facto one. But why should the universe be such as to provide full intellectual satisfaction to its intelligent inhabitants?[15] One may fully concede the "contingency" of the universe, in the sense of its lack of an overall explanation, without believing that such an explanation must at least ideally exist. Indeed, for some existentialist philosophers, contingency by its very nature excludes the existence of transcendent necessity. To Maurice Merleau-Ponty the gratuitousness of existence is an ultimate fact. Any explanation of it is useless since it presupposes the contingency which is to be explained; it also is contradictory since it establishes a necessity whereby the contingent ceases to be contingent. Merleau-Ponty uses the term contingency in a way essentially different from that of the argument, meaning not a being that does not have its ultimate ground in itself, but one that by definition has no ground whatever.[16] Nevertheless, I consider his position significant for the present discussion insofar as it illustrates that to view the universe in terms of the opposition contingent-necessary, is itself already a fundamental philosophical option, and one which is not without alternatives.

### Must the Necessary Being Be Perfect?

If we were able to overcome all those difficulties and to conclude to the existence of a transcendent necessity, we would still need to ensure that this necessary being is God. Yet this appears to be equally difficult. It is, of course, well known that Kant directed his main attack against the transition from necessary to perfect Being. Subsequent interpretations of the argument all bear the impact of this attack. We might paraphrase Kant's critique as follows: Since we lack all empirical evidence concerning the content of the necessary being, we must look for another concept presumably better known that would include the note of necessity. Indeed, although Kant does not mention it, there may be more such concepts. The only known candidate for this role is the concept of the perfect Being. Yet how can I be certain that the concept of the perfect Being is adequate to that of necessary existence? Only by showing that the concept of perfect Being cannot be conceived without the note of necessary existence. But, Kant claims, this evidence can be obtained only by way of the much criticized ontological argument: the nature of the perfect Being is such that it must necessarily exist. Then, since there can be only one absolutely necessary being, by simple conversion I call it perfect. The argument, of course, can be no stronger than the ontological one on which it is based.

Kant's critique is subtle and has been interpreted in various ways. One group of commentators regard the transition to perfect Being as nothing more than a blatant attempt to derive existence directly from a concept. A necessary being in this reading is one whose existence cannot be denied without logical contradiction.

Thus Paul Edwards writes: "To say that there is a necessary being is to say that it would be contradictory to deny its existence. This would mean that at least one existential statement is a necessary truth; and this in turn presupposes that in at least one case existence is contained in a concept.[17] Of course this *is* the ontological argument. As Edwards presents it, the existence of a necessary being is exclusively based on the analysis of a concept. All interpreters who define as necessary only that which cannot be denied without contradictions end up with the same conclusion. Against the validity of such a concept of necessary being militates the obvious fact that sensible people have denied the existence of God and continue to do so without being obviously trapped in a contradiction. Indeed, the contradiction, according to them, is all on the side of those who hold the concept of God. For since no existential being can claim this kind of logical necessity, the proposition: A being necessarily exists, is itself contradictory. Findlay at one time concluded from this fact that therefore God (i.e., the necessary being) cannot exist.[18] The very notion of a self-explanatory being is absurd according to Terence Penelhum.[19]

Even among those who accept no other than a logical necessity at least two have come to the rescue of the argument against this sort of attacks. J.J.C. Smart has pointed out that the existence of a necessary being has not been attained through a mere conversion of the ontological proposition ("the perfect being necessarily exists"), but has been established *before* the transition to the necessary being is made. Consequently, the illegitimate eduction of existence out of a mere concept, the basic logical flaw of the ontological argument, does not take place here.[20] Nevertheless, the basic difficulty with the notion of a being whose non-existence would be logically contradictory remains the same as the one with the ontological argument: existence or non-existence can never be a matter of *logical* necessity.

Alvin Plantinga has attempted to avoid this difficulty by defining as necessary a being that allows no ulterior questions about its existence.[21] Such a necessity might still be called logical even though the proposition which expresses it is non-analytic and consequently can be denied without logical contradiction.

With this definition we are only one step removed from St.

Thomas' own, which, as Peter Geach has pointed out, is not the property of a proposition but the quality of a being that contains no principle of substantial alteration. Since this definition still allows for the possibility of dependent *necessary* beings, one or more necessary beings must be totally self-sufficient and therefore *absolutely* necessary. The argument deals with the latter. Its status differs from that of the propositional necessity in that it does not include existence except in a hypothetical way. *If* it exists it contains no principle of non-existence and will therefore always exist, but if it does not exist, it will never since it is by definition independent.[22] The criticism of the ontological argument does not apply here. For whether such a necessary being exists must be established by inference based upon observation, not by mere analysis of a concept.

Nevertheless, if this necessary being must be further identified as the perfect being in order to be equated with the God of religion, we face the most resistant difficulty of the ontological argument again. For the crucial question of the notion of perfect being is whether it is a valid one, i.e., whether its characteristics are mutually compatible. This, I believe, is a far greater difficulty of the ontological argument than the predication of existence. Yet about the validity of the concept of subsistent perfection the cosmological argument teaches us nothing. It is meaningless, then, to equate the necessary being with the perfect being, if the latter term remains as empty as the former. In the uncritical equation of the two terms the cosmological argument shows a similarity with the ontological one.

However, as I see it, the transition to a perfect being at the end of the cosmological argument is not made because of any conscious or unconscious reference to the ontological argument. It is rather, I suspect, because the idea of a perfect being is the most obvious one to come to the Western mind. For to the Christian, the Jew and the Moslem, God is, above all, perfect. The notion of a perfect being is taken for granted in the argument, because of its unquestioned acceptance by the religious community. Christians, Jews and Moslems feel confident that they know what they are talking about when using this expression. They may well be right. Yet an argument which claims to be a sufficient proof of the existence of God should by no means be allowed to accept uncritically so fundamental a concept.

We may extend this criticism to the usage of the idea of God in most of modern philosophy. Philosophers have been far too much inclined to identify whatever supreme principle their systems happened to require with the God of the Judeo-Christian faith. Descartes' philosophy eloquently illustrates this point. He needed a supreme principle to support the trustworthiness of clear and distinct ideas and to set the mechanical process of nature in motion. He proved to his own satisfaction that such a principle existed, then, without further ado identified it with the Christian God. This transition, while being logically unjustified, also distorted the Judeo-Christian notion of God. Gilson calls Descartes' "author of nature" a stillborn God. "He could not possibly live because, as Descartes had conceived him, he was the God of Christianity reduced to the condition of philosophical principle, in short, an infelicitous hybrid of religious faith and rational thought."[23] To define God as the author of nature is to tie him to nature, and this is only one step from Spinoza's identification, *Deus sive natura*.[24]

Of course, the same mysterious transition, "quod omnes dicunt Deum esse," appears in each of the "ways" of St. Thomas. But Thomas' goal may have been more modest. He does not claim to construe a full-fledged, religious concept of God without any reference to his faith. As a religious believer he attempts to give some rational justification to what he believes. For this purpose he posits various qualities which he finds in the God of his faith and sets out to prove, one by one, that there is a Being which possesses these qualities. The notions of first cause or necessary being are such "stages" in the rational understanding of the God of the religious experience, but no claims of a purely rational definition of God are made for them. Even taken collectively the "ways" do not claim to build a rationally independent idea of God: they merely justify rationally some of the attributes of the God of faith.[25]

Contemporary proponents of the argument appear to return to this more modest approach. Thus F. R. Tennant in his celebrated *Natural Theology* suggested that philosophical speculation about "God" should remain independent of the religious view altogether. The outcome of a philosophical argument, then, may have only the name in common with the God of faith. But the risk of a dual concept, according to Tennant, is preferable to that of an irrational leap in what claims to be a rational argument.[26] One is left to wonder, however, what justifies a name if not the establishment of some connection between the two intended realities.

Another way of dealing with the objection would be to declare the notion of necessary being essentially incomplete though sufficient to meet the basic purpose of the argument. Thus, according to Bruce Reichenbach, the cosmological argument intends only to prove that a necessary being exists, not what properties it possesses. As long as it legitimately concludes to the existence of a being distinct from all contingent and dependent beings, its task would be accomplished.[27] We may then further compare this concept with the religious notion of God by investigating whether the characteristics of the latter include those of the former and in no way contradict them. But this remains outside the scope of the argument proper.

Such a method appears to be unobjectionable. Yet it leaves open the possibility of alternatives and thereby renders the argument inconclusive. A God conceived as necessary being would indeed provide the necessity to support the apparent contingency. Yet there may exist other possibilities. If the principle of absolute necessity is to be identified with the God of faith, we must first prove that the universe as a whole cannot provide its own necessity and then that God is the only possible transcendent necessary being. Neither one of these tasks has been accomplished to everyone's satisfaction.

Yet another attempt has been made to prove the existence of God as the final condition of the intelligibility of the universe by Thomists who were keenly aware of the questionable status of the notion of causality in a transcendent usage and of the difficulty of establishing the presence of actual contingency. The argument uses the comparison of the degrees of perfection on which St. Thomas builds his fourth way. Since it originates in the same search of the ultimate intelligibility of the universe, it may rightfully be presumed to belong to the cosmological argument. All the more so since its contemporary proponents find in this version of the fourth way the support of which the previous two ways stood in need after Kant's attack.[28]

## Absolute Perfection and the Dynamism of the Mind

The reasoning process according to which the very recognition of the finite and the imperfect requires the existence of an infinite, absolutely perfect Being is not discussed as a separate argument by Kant. One might therefore be inclined to assume that it escapes his critique. But far from being the case this argument more than the others is at odds with the basic principles of Kant's critique. It most overtly violates Kant's prohibition to go from the phenomenal to the noumenal. Nevertheless it deserves attentive scrutiny, for the argument of degrees of perfection has been most carefully developed by scholars who remained acutely aware of Kant's objections.

First let us consider its early, pre-Kantian formulation.

Among beings there are some more and some less good, true, noble and the like. But *more* and *less* are predicated of different things according as they resemble in their different ways something which is the maximum, as a thing is said to be hotter according as it more nearly resembles that which is hottest. . . . Now the maximum in any genus is the cause of all in that genus, as fire which is the maximum of heat, is the cause of all hot things, as is said in the same book (*Metaphysics*, II). Therefore there must also be something which is to all beings the cause of their being, goodness, and every other perfection; and this we call God.[29]

The argument as it stands here appears to consist of a combination of the Platonic theory of participation and of efficient causality. In Thomas the supreme exemplar must also be the first cause: a perfection which does not coincide with the being which possesses it must have been caused by the being which fully realizes it.[30] Yet is it not evident that the argument requires this connection with causality. Contemporary Scholastics have used it to provide the proof of causality with a more solid basis. We shall discuss them in a moment. Meanwhile let us mention a basic objection against the common form of the argument.

What is a maximum? Assuming that indeed we can perceive a scale of perfection only against the backdrop of a maximal realization of this perfection (a very risky assumption, since a comparison between any two realizations would seem to do as well), we must still face the question whether this maximum is also the maximum *possible*. Saint Thomas clearly assumes that this must be the case, but he fails to prove it and I do not believe that it can be proven without a complete acceptance of Plato's theory that to every imperfect reality corresponds an *ideal actuality*.[31]

Yet the argument must be defended against the absurdities to which an indiscriminate concept of perfection would lead. Although Thomas mentions fire as "the maximum of heat," Plato's own criticism should warn us that the theory applies only to so-called transcendental or ontological qualities which contain no formal imperfection, as physical qualities inevitably do. Being a blonde may be a perfection in an attractive woman, yet it excludes her from the aesthetic perfection of a brunette. On the other hand, one may well wonder whether such transcendental perfections as being, truth and goodness are not too common to allow any substantial realization. If anything that is is "being," what would pure being possibly mean? For goodness and truth we face the additional difficulty that they must be conceived as determinations of the mind. Thus the maximum of truth could only be what the mind conceives irrefutably to be the case. It is not immediately evident why this should be God.

Modern versions of the argument are mostly based upon an article by Joseph Lemaitre, an author of the Louvain school of Thomism.[32] According to Lemaitre the affirmation of the limited reality as such requires the horizon of the unlimitedly real. Variations of this principle are found over the entire history of philosophy. That the finite can be perceived as finite only against the background of infinity is the key to Descartes' proof for the existence of God in the third of his *Meditations*. Challenged on this point Descartes attacked the objection of his critics that the idea of the infinite Being could be a merely negative concept, a denial of limitations. According to him, the idea of infinity is prior to that of the finite.

> I must not imagine that I do not apprehend the infinite by a true idea, but only by the negation of the finite, in the same way that I comprehend repose and darkness by the negation of motion and light: since, on the contrary, I clearly perceive that there is more reality in the infinite substance than in the finite, and therefore that in some way I possess the perception of the infinite before that of the finite, that is, the perception of God before that of myself.[33]

Yet Lemaitre and the followers of Marechal gave the argument a Kantian twist which was absent from the earlier versions. According to them, the need to assume a maximum in the scale of being (if such a need exists) would have its basis, not in the nature of the finite as such, but in the nature of the mind. Most of their efforts were spent on proving the existence of an impetus toward the absolute, either in the order of the intellect or, resuming Blondel's line of thinking, in the will.

Auguste Grégoire, for instance, argues that the implicit affirmation of unlimited Being provides a necessary element for the mental constitution of the object as such. This is an attempt to reply in Kant's own terms to the Kantian objection that the constitution of empirical objects in no way requires an absolute reality and, consequently, that its affirmation is a matter of pure speculation with no basis in fact. "The relation to the absolute is not added to objects already constituted, as Kant thought: it is an intrinsic or constitutive element of the object as such."[34] From the affirmation of unlimited being in each cognitive act Marechal's followers conclude that the adequate object of the intellect is the idea of God.[35]

Among contemporary authors the necessity of an infinite horizon for the perception of the finite, was most forcefully asserted by Rahner and Lonergan.[36] I have discussed Rahner's position elsewhere and shall therefore restrict my remarks to Lonergan. His argument as it appears in *Insight* may be formalized as follows. *If the real is completely intelligible, God exists. But the real is com-*

*pletely intelligible. Therefore, God exists.* A conditional sorites proves the major premise. If the real is completely intelligible, then complete intelligibility exists. (For the real is all that is to be affirmed, and to affirm it is to know it to exist.) If complete intelligibility exists, the idea of Being exists. (For the idea of Being is the only one that is completely intelligible: it is the all-inclusive end of the mind's unrestricted desire to know.) If the idea of Being exists, God exists. (For the primary component of the idea of Being possesses all the attributes of what we call God.) The minor premise is proven: the real is all that is to be affirmed, and if the affirmation is universal its name is Being. Lonergan answers the Kantian objection that an unrestricted act of understanding may well be impossible by stating that the unlimited *desire* to understand is not an ideal but a fact and his argument is exclusively based on this fact. I do not believe that this takes care of the entire difficulty, for the fact of an unlimited desire to know does not necessarily imply the *ultimate* intelligibility of the real (granting that it calls for an unlimited intelligibility). Moreover, the identification of Being with complete intelligibility depends upon philosophical principles to which no Kantian would subscribe. However, it appears unnecessary to enter further into this unusually complex argument, since Lonergan's later development which we shall have an opportunity to discuss makes a critique of his early position superfluous.

A similar argument could be made on the basis of the mind's unlimited striving for value. Thus Maurice Blondel discovers the transcendent in the impetus of human action rather than in the dynamism of the intellect. Through action freedom brings the physical world under control. Yet conquest of the world is not man's deepest concern. His real objective is self-transcendence. The living impulse toward action surpasses all actual and possible achievements and intends a transphenomenal, absolute reality. "All attempts to bring human action to completion fail, and yet human action cannot but strive to complete itself and to suffice to itself. It must but it cannot. The feeling of impotence as well as that of the need for an infinite consummation remains incurable."[37] The impetus of freedom in the heart of all human action reveals an infinite reality. For only an infinite reality could keep human action moving beyond all finite goals.[38] All the previous difficulties return when Blondel attempts to identify the transcendent horizon of human striving with God. Undoubtedly, the awareness of finitude reveals a transcendence, a beyond-the-limit. But the whole problem is how to give this transcendent a positive content which makes it into something more than a mere "beyond." The limit experience as such does not provide a content. The act of faith, which provides a content, may use the limit experience but is in no way implied in it. The limit experience may be the occasion to discover a deeper, hidden reality.[39] But this does not always happen and there is no intrinsic necessity in the nature of the experience itself that it should.

I do not want to deny at this point that the finite is not intelligible to the human mind without the infinite. But either this principle remains purely philosophical, and then it provides no positive content to the infinite horizon; or the infinite is given a religious content, and then the term "intelligible" is no longer used in the strictly philosophical sense. Even the thesis that the universe as a whole (rather than particular objects in it) is finite, states not a simple fact but a choice of perspective which may be religiously necessary but which is not philosophically inevitable. I see no compelling reason to consider the universe finite even if science were to prove that its spatial and its temporal dimensions can be comprehended in finite numbers. If one defines as infinite what is not limited by another thing of the same nature, as Spinoza did,[40] this universe is infinite, regardless of its dimensions. On the other hand, from a religious perspective it makes good sense to call even a spatially and temporally unlimited universe finite.

The true meaning of the argument of the degrees of perfection, then, is that it is not a proof, but a logical articulation of the religious way of looking at the world. Religious is he who sees the universe as finite *because* he sees it in the infinite.[41] This, in fact, is the essence of the religious vision of the world. It escapes the faulty juxtaposition of the finite and the infinite which Hegel denounced in the structure of all proofs for the existence of God. From a religious perspective the finite is *in* the infinite, because the infinite is *prior* to the finite. But this vision is lost as soon as the infinite is presented as logically or epistemologically implied in the perception of the finite.

The mind explores the horizon of knowing and doing in different and irreducible ways. Science and philosophy, artistic creation, moral achievement, all reveal in their own way the existence of an ideal boundary of knowledge and action, an "unknown known" which the mind cognitively intends without comprehending it.[42] The religious intentionality differs from all other forms of self-transcendence in that it gives a positive content to what in all other respects must remain transcendent. Thus it appears to achieve what the philosophical view of the horizon merely initiates.

The philosopher will find it hard to argue for or against such claims, but he will insist that they cannot be considered scientific. To him all this must remain *docta ignorantia*. Yet he cannot but follow with interest the attempts to explore the transcendent horizon made through other avenues than his own.

## NOTES

1. Albert Michotte, *The Perception of Causality*, trans. by T.R. and Elaine Miles (London, Methuen, 1963).
2. *An Enquiry concerning Human Understanding*, IV, 1, ed. by L.A. Selby-Bigge (Oxford: Clarendon, 1888), p. 28.
3. *Critique of Pure Reason*, A 609 Transl. Norman Kemp Smith (New York: Macmillan, 1965), p. 511.
4. It should be pointed out that competent proponents of the argument such as Copleston, Mascall and Grégoire have been aware of this difficulty and distinguish a metaphysical or vertical causality from a descriptive or horizontal one. Yet the question remains whether the former is a viable concept.
5. Thus, Bertrand Russell in his essay "On the Notion of Cause" in *Our Knowledge of the External World* (New America Library, 1963), p. 25.
6. Bruce Reichenbach, *The Cosmological Argument* (Springfield, Charles C. Thomas, 1972), p. 47.
7. The most sophisticated version of this argument of intelligibility is the one provided by Bernard Lonergan in *Insight* (New York: Philosophical Library, 1967), p. 654-55.
8. F.C. Copleston in his debate with Bertrand Russell on the existence of God, in John Hick, *The Existence of God* (New York: Macmillan, 1972), p. 173-74.
9. "Arguments for the Existence of God" in *The Journal of Theological Studies* 40 (1939), p. 26.
10. Russell summarizes the point well: "The whole concept of cause

is one we derive from our observation of particular things; I see no reason whatsoever to suppose that the total has any cause whatsoever." (*Op. cit.*, p. 175.)

11. Critics of Thomas' argument would do well to heed this distinction. One commentator blunts a number of attacks by his conclusion: "Aquinas did not hold either that everything in the natural world is contingent, or that a necessary being is one which cannot possibly not-exist, or that any being which is necessary must be the *ens realissimum* or *perfectissimum.*" Patterson Brown, "St. Thomas' Doctrine of Necessary Being," *The Philosophical Review* 73 (1946), p. 82. Cf. also Anthony Kenny, *The Five Ways* (London: Routledge and Kegan Paul, 1969), p. 49-53.

12. *Summa Theologiae* 1, 2, 3.

13. Auguste Grégoire, *Immanence et Transcendance* (Brussels, 1963), p. 47.

14. *Arguments for the Existence of God* (New York: Macmillan, 1970), p. 48.

15. This is the core of C.D. Broad's critique of the causal argument. "Arguments for the Existence of God" *The Journal of Theological Studies* 40 (1939), pp. 27-28.

16. Cf. William A. Luypen, *Phenomenology and Atheism* (Pittsburgh: Duquesne University Press, 1964), pp. 308-14.

17. "The Cosmological Argument" in *The Cosmological Arguments*, ed. by Donald R. Burrill (New York: Doubleday, 1967), p. 116.

18. J.N. Findlay, "Can God's Existence Be Disproved?" in *Mind* (1948) reprinted in *New Essays in Philosophical Theology*, ed. by Flew & MacIntyre.

19. Terrence Penelhum "Divine Necessity" in *The Cosmological Arguments*, pp. 151-55.

20. J.J.C. Smart, "The Existence of God" in *New Essays in Philosophical Theology*, ed. by A. Flew and A. MacIntyre (New York: Macmillan, 1964), pp. 36-37.

21. "Necessary Being" in *Faith and Philosophy*, ed. by Alvin Plantinga (Grand Rapids, 1964), pp. 97-108. For a somewhat similar position, cf. R.L. Franklin, "Necessary Being" in *Australasian Journal of Philosophy* 35 (1957), pp. 97-110.

22. I owe this formulation to Bruce Reichenbach, *The Cosmological Argument*, p. 118.

23. Etienne Gilson, *God and Philosophy* (New Haven: Yale University Press, 1959), p. 89.

24. Descartes himself anticipated this in his first definition of nature: "By nature, considered in general, I am now understanding nothing else than either God, or the order and the disposition established by God in related things." *Méditations, Oeuvres*, ed. Adam-Tannery (Paris, 1897-1913), Vol. IX, p. 64.

25. Cf. Edward Sillem, *Ways of Thinking About God* (New York: Sheed and Ward, 1960), pp. 76, 175.

26. *Philosophical Theology* (Cambridge University Press, 1935), Vol. II, pp. 78-79.

27. *Op. cit.*, pp. 131-34.

28. Thus Auguste Grégoire, *Immanence et transcendance* (Brussels, 1939). Also, Bernard Lonergan, *Insight*, Ch. 19. Joseph Maréchal in his *Point de départ de la métaphysique*, Cahier V (Louvain), follows the same line of reasoning without claiming to present an argument for the existence of God.

29. St. Thomas, *Summa Theologiae* I, qu. 2, a.3.

30. On the connection between exemplary and efficient causality in the fourth way, cf. Gerard Smith, S.J., *Natural Theology* (New York: Macmillan, 1951), p. 131.

31. Cf. also Anthony Kenny, *op. cit.*, p. 81.

32. "La preuve de l'existence de Dieu par les degrés de l'être" in *Nouvelle Revue Théologique*, 54 (1927), pp. 321 ff, 436 ff.

33. *Oeuvres*, ed. Adam-Tannery, Vol. VII, p. 45; *Meditations*, trans. by John Veitch, in *The Rationalists* (New York: Doubleday, s.d.), p. 137.

34. *Immanence et transcendance*, p. 121.

35. *Op. cit.*, p. 124.

36. The studies on the religious experience by Johannes B. Lotz and Hans Ogiermann must be read in the same tradition. Although they do not give arguments for the existence of God, they also view the affirmation of Being. For Lotz the religious experience is implied in the metaphysical grasp of Being and completes it. For Ogiermann the religious insight is similar to the metaphysical, even though the two experiences are independent. Cf. Johannes Lotz, "Zur Struktur der religiösen Erfahrung" in *Interpretation der Welt*, ed. H. Kuhn, H. Kahlefeld, K. Forster (Wurzburg, 1964), pp. 205-226. J. Lotz, "Metaphysische und religiöse Erfahrung" in *Archivio di Filosofia*, I (1956), pp. 79-121. H. Ogiermann, "Die Problematik der religiösen Erfahrung" in *Scholastik*, 37 (1962), pp. 481-513.

37. *L'action* (1893) (Paris, 1950), p. 321.

38. For a more extensive discussion of the transition from the ideal to the real in Blondel's *L'action*, cf. Chapter 5.

39. See Romano Guardini, *Religion und Offenbarung*, I, p. 84.

40. *Ethics*, Bk. I, def. 2 and proposition 8.

41. " 'Finite,' as the Thomist uses it, is naturally understood by contrast with 'infinite' as this latter term is applied to God. To say the world is finite is to say that it is limited, *as God is unlimited*, that it cannot account for its own existence, *as God can account for his*, etc. Thus, from the Thomist point of view, to say 'The world is finite'—*really meaning what you say*—may be precisely to say 'There is an Infinite Being.' " Thomas McPherson, *The Philosophy of Religion* (New York: Van Nostrand, 1965), pp. 60-61.

42. This line of thinking was mainly pursued by Bernard Lonergan in his recent work. For an illuminating discussion of this theme in his work, cf. David W. Tracy, *The Achievement of Bernard Lonergan* (New York: Herder, 1970), pp. 169-182, 206-231. Also by the same author, "Horizon Analysis and Eschatology" in *Continuum* (1968), pp. 169, 172.

# 8
# The Teleological Argument

The argument of design is not a single, homogeneous structure. Kant, who was familiar only with a modern version, referred to it as the oldest proof for the existence of God. Old it is indeed, even though we do not have evidence of its use as a "proof" until Philo. Although Aristotle was the one who developed the very concept of teleology on which all later arguments would be based, he himself used the argument in none of his extant works: the process of adaptation is a work of nature rather than of God.[1] Even to the Stoics the idea of an ordered cosmos ruled by a divine Providence was more a theological conclusion than a philosophical premise. Instead of "proving" the presence of a divine Logos in the world, they rather attempted to justify this assumed presence in the face of objections of disorder. Today we would not term such an attempt natural theology but theodicy. Philo, from all appearances, based his argument on Aristotle's lost dialogue.[2] The argument as he uses it places most of the emphasis on the harmony in the universe. Later Aristotle's teleological considerations also would be developed into a full-fledged argument. Occasionally the two would run parallel, at other times they would merge. Since this article does not intend to be historical, I omit here the complex development of the two forms and merely take an example of each from Aquinas who gave both their distinct expressions for many centuries. However, since I intend to deal primarily with the contemporary discussion, I shall not restrict myself to that early expression or concern myself with its historical circumstances. First, I shall consider the proof based on the existence of ends, then the one based on the order in the universe.

## The Teleological Argument

In the *Summa Theologiae* Thomas writes:

We see that things which lack knowledge, such as natural bodies act for an end, and this is evident from their acting always, or nearly always, in the same way, so as to obtain the best result. Hence it is plain that they achieve their end, not fortuitously, but designedly. Now whatever lacks knowledge cannot move toward an end, unless it be directed by some being endowed with knowledge and intelligence; as the arrow is directed by the archer. Therefore some intelligent being exists by whom all natural things are directed to their end: and this being we call God.[3]

Two things are affirmed here. One, the constancy of relations and the general direction indicate the presence of a teleological directedness in nature. Two, such a directedness must be the work of a mind. Obviously the term *end* is to be understood here as the purpose which motivates the development, not as the actual outcome of a process. Yet the difficulty consists in detecting the presence of a purpose when we only have direct access to the outcome. We are clearly not justified to conclude to the former merely because we find some meaning in the latter. For as every conceivable state of affairs, even one resulting from the merest fortuitous coincidence, may be interpreted as a meaningful outcome, one could attribute purpose to every process.

Nor do repetition and regularity necessarily indicate the presence of purpose, since a particular system may perpetuate itself if the factor which disturbs it entails an element that will restore the original state. Predictability, then, is no indication of teleological directedness. Neither is the mere fact that certain events condition the occurrence of other events. The ecological cycle of nature appears to be a marvelously coherent system. But must we regard it as a teleological process? Not necessarily, for the outcome in this case may not be more than the balance finally attained among conflicting elements. Moreover, which state would be the "end" of the system?

Can we ever conclude from the nature of the outcome and the development of the process to the presence of a purpose? Rigorist interpreters would claim that only acts of beings that are capable of belief and desire may safely be termed purposive.[4] If correct, this conclusion would deprive the argument of all its power, since the existence of such a being is precisely what must be proven. Others, such as C. A. Mace, have been more optimistic about the possibility of detecting teleological characteristics in the process itself.[5] Yet then the second question emerges: Must such a process necessarily be the work of a mind? Mace believes that it is at least highly probable that a teleological process defined in his terms occurs only where a mind is operative. In any event, the attribution of a teleological directedness to beings other than man and perhaps some higher animals cannot be fully verified. At best a teleological explanation of certain types of behavior may be empirically more satisfactory than a nonteleological.[6]

The advent of Darwin's theory has, of course, considerably contributed to the demise of teleological speculations. Yet in the final analysis, Darwinism neither adds to, nor subtracts from, the essence of the original teleological argument. Its strength and weakness fall entirely outside its scope. Nevertheless a frequent presentation of the argument from the seventeenth century onward is very much open to Darwin's attacks. For any adaptation of a particular animal to its environment or of an organ to a particular function may be the outcome of an elimination process rather than of a teleological development. This applies to William Paley's famous description of the functioning of the eye[7] and to Hume's argument based on the complimentarity of male and female for generative purposes in anatomy, passion, and instinct. Those arguments lose their power once the adaption is no longer conceived as an instant fact but as the outcome of a long and often devious evolutionary process. Darwin clearly anticipated the catastrophic impact which his theory would have on the traditional argument. "The old argument of design in nature, as given by Paley, which formally seemed to me so conclusive, fails, now that the law of natural selection has been discovered. We can no longer argue that, for instance, the beautiful hinge of a bivalve shell must have been made by an intelligent being, like the hinge of a door by man."[8] The relation between the final outcome of an evolutionary process and the various stages leading to it is quite different from the one between end and means in the production of an artifact. Out of a number of mutations only those are preserved which enhance the individual's chances for survival in a particular environment. There is natural selection but no evidence of choice.[9]

Paradoxically Darwin and his followers continue to use teleological models of interpretation. The very term "natural selection," derived from cattle breeding, connotes a preexisting design as well as certain principles of economy in the execution of this design. Susanne Langer has rightly criticized this terminology. "So all the considerations of economy, time-saving, margins of safety, reserves of material, storage and deployment of power, and the principles of coordination and communication governing our industry are read into the organic forms and functions that have taken shape in the course of evolution."[10] The problems are increased by the fact that selection strongly evokes the idea of an intelligent agent. Darwin and his successors no longer refer to God as the supreme planner but they ascribe to "Nature" or "Evolution" pretty much the same function.

This is much more than a matter of linguistic accuracy, for the teleological implications may lead us to anticipate developments which are not borne out by the facts. Thus on the basis of a teleological interpretation one would expect only those variations (mutations in Neo-Darwinism) to become permanent which contribute to the species' survival. But no evidence at all supports such a Leibnizian economy of perfection. A number of mutations are retained which fulfill no function whatever. The question clearly is not what "Nature" requires for its future perfection but what the present situation allows. This situation displays neither design nor perfection, except perhaps in the highly qualified sense which I shall discuss soon. Instead of a preexisting plan which tolerates no deviation, we only find undetermined impulses which are able or unable to assert themselves in a given environment. Such a view of evolution differs substantially from the common one which appears to be guided by what one critic has called "the myth of the maximum," according to which the promotion of the ultimate end must be maximized. That only those acts which will yield a higher production than their alternatives will be chosen, may be validly assumed in economy. But nothing in the evolutionary process justifies the assumption that the fitness standard will be maximized. What remains is "not the best, but only the better, the good enough, the temporary expedient."[11] The "economic" teleology holds no basis in fact but only in an anthropomorphic, teleological model. In a complex system of agents various forms of interplay lead to different results and only those results will be preserved which are not neutralized by opposite components. Thus, compared to its antecedents, the outcome "makes sense" and our tendency to give it a teleological interpretation becomes understandable enough.

Yet the evolution theory has not necessarily eliminated the possibility of a teleological worldview. For as long as no purposive intervention is required for any particular adaptation the argument still stands. As Anthony Kenny remarks "The argument was only that the ultimate explanation of such adaptation must be found in intelligence; and if the argument was correct, then any Darwinian success merely inserts an extra step between the phenomena to be explained and their ultimate explanation."[12]

Indeed, far from diminishing the possibility of a teleological world order, one might claim with Anthony Flew that the evolution theory has brought just so much more grist to the mill of the teleologist.[13] In the new context of the object of teleological speculation will be the consistent, one-dimensional trend of a development which, for all we know, is not the only possible one: an evolution toward ever greater complexity and deeper inwardness ultimately resulting in the improbable event of life. The development has continued to move toward the most complex forms of life and from all appearances it still has not completed its course. Why, out of an infinite number of possibilities, were just the conditions of life fulfilled, and fulfilled almost at once?[14] Their fulfillment cannot be explained by a biological struggle for survival.[15] Everything seems to have been "arranged" toward the development of consciousness, although an almost infinite number of complex factors were needed for this *involution*. Individually all these steps can be explained without invoking teleology. But considering the steady development of the process toward greater complexity, the observer inevitably receives the impression that the evolution moves toward a specific goal. Still, no empirical evidence can ever establish more than a more or less steady development in one direction. Whether this directedness be interpreted in a teleological sense or not, depends on the philosophical inclinations of the observer, but it can never be considered a strictly scientific conclusion. From the same facts and even theories which led Teilhard de Chardin and Lecomte du Nouy to a teleological interpretation, Monod and Rostand conclude, to a purely deterministic, nonteleological one.

Even if a compelling case could be made for the teleological view, the existence of a perfect designer would not necessarily follow. For to warrant such a conclusion the evolutionary process would have to appear *evidently* good. But who could claim this for a development in which individuals and entire species are sacrificed? The end result is the outcome of a long and cruel struggle which left most of the participants dead by the roadside. From the victims' point of view at least there would be little perfection in the alleged ends-means relation of the present arrangement. That man, who came as the winner out of this contest, considers himself the goal of the development and imposes his own purposes upon all of organic and inorganic nature, is understandable enough. In one sense such a view is also correct, for only a person can conceive of himself as a purpose and once he has started doing so is no longer able to see himself as subordinate to any other part of nature. But does the ultimacy of man's position indicate the existence of a perfect design? Could mind itself not be an abortive attempt, a terminus of the evolutionary drive, that is doomed to extinction? Behavioral scientists wonder more and more whether man will be able to survive his built-in problems.[16] Not only psychologists but also biologists (e.g., Paul Maclean) begin to question how man can continue to live with the schizoid nature that is his. Without considering these pessimistic forecasts, we may still wonder whether the record of his actual achievements, past and present, justifies the assumption of a vast and complex creation by an all-wise God. The unprejudiced mind finds it difficult to detect a divine purpose in man's accomplishments. Even Hegel, so incorrigibly optimistic in his philosophy of history, wrote at the end of his life:

We see the earth covered with ruins, with remains of the splendid edifices and works left by the finest nations whose ends we recognize as having a substantial value. Great national objects and human works do indeed endure and defy time, but all that splendid national life has irrecoverably perished. We thus see how, on the one hand, petty, subordinate, even despicable designs are fulfilled; and, on the other hand, how those which are recognized as having substantial value are frustrated.[17]

Yet, one might object with Kant, even if man would never accomplish anything else, he could still be the *moral* purpose of the universe. In his *Critique of Judgment* Kant claims that the universe finds its ultimate purpose not in man's cognitive or technical needs or in his pleasure, but in his moral will which alone is an unconditioned end.[18] Only the moral will of man could give a Supreme Being a sufficient reason for creating a world. Kant is not disturbed by man's apparent wickedness, for morality, being purely internal, need not be an external success. Nevertheless, Kant himself had to postulate an afterlife in order to give the will the holiness which it is unable to attain in this life and which alone makes man a worthy purpose of the universe. Thus teleological considerations determine the meaning of the ethical postulate of the existence of God. But they were never adequate to become an argument.

In summary, I do not see how any teleological speculations could provide us with an "argument" for the existence of a perfect Designer. A person may draw his own conclusions from whatever private insights he has in this domain, but none of those can claim the universality of a compelling reason.

## The Argument of Order

Let us now turn toward the concept of *order*. In the *Summa contra gentiles* Thomas writes: "In the world we find that things of diverse natures come together under one order, and this not rarely or by chance, but always or for the most part. There must therefore be some being by whose providence the world is governed."[19] The preceding concept of "end" is closely connected with the concept of "order" because a coordination of ends and means always presupposes some order among things. Yet order could conceivably exist without end-means relations. Moreover, when teleological relations do obtain within the universe, the universe itself cannot simply be conceived in terms of end and means. I even suspect that teleological considerations become meaningless when applied to entire organisms within the universe. What could possibly be the "purpose" of a plant or an animal? To refer to them in such a manner is merely a crudely anthropomorphic way of saying that man uses them for his own benefit. At any rate, the term purpose does not apply to the universe as a whole, certainly not in the way in which end-means relations obtain *within* the world.

Another reason for distinguishing order from teleology is that the former appears to escape the specific criticisms to which the latter is subject. There is no question here of the adaptation of individual means to individual ends, or even of an ultimate purpose of all processes. The basic observation here is that the impression of order is not restricted to the production of life from inorganic matter. Even in its static appearance the world seems to be an organized whole rather than a random collection of diverse and unrelated beings.

The concept of order refers to any disposition of elements which allows the mind to recognize the totality of them as an intelligible, aesthetic, or moral unity. Man has always perceived the world as a *cosmos*, to which the structures of the mind can be applied. But what is the significance of this fact? Does the coordination of physical phenomena and mental structures imply that the universe was "designed" by a mind similar to our own? Hardly. Structures are invented by the mind in accordance with its need to comprehend the universe as it in fact appears to us. Mathematical concepts apply to the world not because of a preestablished divine harmony between the mind and the world, but because that particular kind of symbolization was developed which proved most useful to understand the given world. Still, one might insist, the applicability of rational models presupposes the existence of a certain amount of coordination in the *real* world. This I fully concede, but, then, a universe without some degree of coordination would not only be unintelligible, it would also be impossible. If a universe exists at all, it must exist in some sort of order. Order is not an additional element, a distinctive ornament of one of the many possible worlds. It is the very condition of existence of a complex totality. We need no different justification for the order in the world than for the existence of the world. In whatever fashion the universe may have originated, a minimum of order had to be present instantly if it was to survive at all. The impossibility of absolute disorder, then, turns out to be the Achilles heel of the argument. For if order is a necessary condition of existence, its presence yields no indication of its origin.

Note well, the dilemma here is not between order and pure chance, as the argument's advocates claim, but between an order imposed from without and one emerging from within. The argument gratuitously assumes that the only possible alternative to blind chance is a transcendent design. The arrangement of diverse things into an orderly pattern cannot result from their own divergent natures, Aquinas claims.[20] But does the arrangement become more intelligible by assuming an orderly principle *above* the universe? Could rationality not have its source *in* the universe? If we accept a universe without beginning, as most Greeks did and as Aquinas himself considered to be irrefutably possible, could the arrangement not be inherent in the totality?

To be sure, the order in the universe impresses us *as if* it had been designed, because in manufactured products order results from design. But for the order of the universe no trace of an actual designer can ever be found and we may be tempted to agree with the skeptic in Wisdom's "Gods," that no gardener is responsible for the garden.[21] What ultimately justifies this skepticism is the well-known difficulty involved in transferring what we know about the origin of an artifact to the origin of the universe. To counter Hume's objection of our inexperience with regard to the origins of worlds, it is insufficient to reply that a perfect analogy exists nowhere and that all reasoning goes beyond actual experience. For the universe is unique in a different way: while all other things are part of it, here the whole, as such, is the very issue.

I repeat, the problem is not whether the existence of order requires an explanation, but whether this explanation must come from within the universe. The principle of an immanent logos becomes absurd only if one previously *assumes* that the universe cannot be intrinsically rational or even divine by itself—as it was for the Greeks. But such an assumption already presupposes the acceptance of the very theism one wants to prove.

However, granting the existence of a designed (i.e., transcendently imposed) order, does the order which actually obtains require a *divine* designer? Certainly not if only a *perfect* order requires a perfect designer. Even if we are willing to assume that an imperfect order might have been designed by a perfect God, it is difficult to conceive how such an imperfect order could provide evidence of a perfect creator unless his existence was already known from other sources. What can we conclude about the nature of the designer on the basis of astral collisions in distant galaxies, natural disasters on a life-bearing planet, the extinction of entire species for lack of a proper environment, the births of monsters and defective individuals, and, among conscious beings, the inestimable amounts of suffering and pain? To be sure, one may still *assume* that the present order is the best possible, as Leibniz did, but there clearly is no evidence that such must be the case. Indeed, the apparent absence of due order has become as much an objection against the acceptance of a perfect creator as the presence of order is an argument in its favor. The basic question, then, is: Is the imperfect order of the actual universe sufficient to prove the existence of a perfect designer? Could a Being of absolute wisdom and almighty power not have prevented some of the disorder? Or, as Bertrand Russell somewhat maliciously put it, do you think that, if you were granted omnipotence and omniscience and millions of years in which to perfect your world, you could produce nothing better than the Ku Klux Klan or the Fascists?[22] The simple answer to this question is that we do not know, because we ignore how much evil *could* have been avoided and how much goodness *could* have been added. But as long as we remain in the dark on those issues, the argument misses a basic premise. We are stranded with the dilemma of a world that is too good for not having been designed at all, and too bad for having obviously been designed by a wise, omnipotent God. Or, as William E. Hocking aptly expressed it:

From the standpoint of naturalism, the world is suprisingly good; from the standpoint of religion, it is surprisingly bad; for naturalism, there is no problem of evil; there is no problem of good—and this problem is the substance of the teleological argument. But from the standpoint of religion, there is a problem of evil; and this problem is the burden of objection to the force of the proof.[23]

## Conclusion

It may be appropriate to conclude this critique with a few remarks on its limitation. I have attempted to show that the argument of design independently of the religious experience is unable to prove the existence of God. Is the man who sees the hand of God in the workings of this universe therefore subject to an illusion? Such a conclusion does not follow from the preceding critique. What was an illusion is the "purely philosophical" status of the teleological argument. But the real thrust of teleological considerations in the religious vision does not lie in their probative power. *If man is religious* he cannot but see order as God's order, and he expresses this in a teleological theology. To him the order of the world, its beauty, its service to man, cease to be gratuitous. All these qualities, whatever their possible explanations may be, find their ultimate resting point in his faith. In this respect the attitude of faith differs substantially from that of philosophy which can make no assumptions that it is unable to justify by logical reflection upon experience. Usually the so-called arguments merely allow the believer to understand what he antecedently believed.[24] In the words of Norman Kemp Smith:

> In and through their religious experience of fellowship with God, they have belief in God, and coming to nature and history with this belief in their minds, they interpret nature and history freely in accordance therewith. They do not observe order and design, and *therefore* infer a Designer: they argue that order and design must be present even when they are not apparent, because all existences other than God have their source in him.[25]

The argument of design draws attention to a specific set of facts in which the religious mind confronts the transcendent.[26] Order and disorder force both believer and nonbeliever beyond the mere acceptance of empirical facts. To religious man, the detection of harmony and purpose becomes an occasion of faith and joy, just as the inability to explain disorder induces religious doubt. (The

Psalms and the Book of Job are eloquent witnesses of both attitudes.) He feels that the nonbeliever is also puzzled by order and disorder, and he wants to communicate his own world view. If he does this by attempting to educe the notion of Supreme Being from the idea of order, he merely commits a logical error. But often he is aware of the restrictions imposed by his particular universe of discourse. Even the much-criticized Paley did not think of himself as "proving" God to someone who had never heard of him, for he admitted that the recognition of divine purpose might require "some previous knowledge of the subject."

## NOTES

1. Two rare instances where God is declared to be responsible for the adaptation are *De Coelo* 271$^a$ 33 and *De Generatione et Corruptione* 336$^b$ 32. W. D. Ross interprets these passages as "a literary device and a concession to ordinary ways of thinking" incompatible with Aristotle's nonintervention theology. See W. D. Ross, *Aristotle* (Boston: Meridian Books, 1959), pp. 81, 176. Yet in Aristotle's lost early work, *On Philosophy,* he clearly introduced the teleological argument. See Werner Jaeger, *Aristotle: Fundamentals of the History of His Development,* trans. R. Robinson, (Oxford, 1948), pp. 159-61; and Anton Hermann Chroust, "A Cosmological Proof for the Existence of God in Aristotle's Lost Dialogue, *On Philosophy,*" *New Scholasticism* 40 (1966): 447-63.

2. *Legum Allegoriarum Libri Tres* III, 32, 97-99; *De Praemiis et Poenis* VII, 41-43.

3. *S.T.* I, 2, 3. Translated as *Basic Writings of St. Thomas,* ed. Anton Pegis (New York: Random House, 1945).

4. C.J. Ducasse, "Explanation, Mechanism and Teleology," *Journal of Philosophy* 23 (1926). Reprinted in *Readings in Philosophical Analysis,* ed. H. Feigl and Wilfred Sellars (New York: Appleton Century, 1949), pp. 540-44.

5. C. A. Mace describes as teleological a process by which a negative condition is counteracted by a contrasting condition in such a way that all action which increases the degree of the latter tends to be continued or repeated, while any action which decreases that degree tends to be discontinued, and that, with repetition of the process, the process as a whole approximates to a set of component actions which performed in that order and only in that order are sufficient to produce the second condition ("Mechanical and Teleological Causation," *Readings in Analytic Philosophy,* pp. 535-36).

6. This is the line of reasoning taken by Charles Taylor, *The Explanation of Behavior* (New York: Humanities Press, 1964).

7. William Paley, *Natural Theology*, ed. Frederick Ferré (Indianapolis: Bobbs-Merrill Co., 1963), pp. 13-19.

8. *Autobiography* (London: Collins, 1958), p. 87.

9. Norman Kemp Smith comments on Darwin's text. "The hinge of a door affords conclusive proof of the existence of an artificer; the hinge of the bivalve shell, though incomparably superior as a hinge, affords no such proof: it is as natural in its origin as anything in physical nature can be known to be" ("Is Divine Existence Credible?" in *The Credibility of Divine Existence* [New York: Saint Martin Press], p. 139).

10. Susanne Langer, *Mind: An Essay on Human Feeling* (Baltimore: Johns Hopkins University Press, 1967), p. 360.

11. William C. Wimsatt, "The Machine in the Ghost" (paper read at the annual meeting of the American Metaphysical Society, Washington, D.C., 1972).

12. Anthony Kenny, *The Five Ways* (London: Routledge & Kegan Paul, 1969).

13. *God and Philosophy* (New York: Harcourt, Brace & World, 1966), p. 60.

14. The appearance of a single molecule of dissymmetry such as those of living organisms is difficult to explain by chance. The appearance of hundreds of millions of them becomes almost impossible.

15. F. R. Tennant made the point well: "Of a struggle for existence between rival worlds, out of which ours has survived as the fittest, we have no knowledge upon which to draw. Natural selection cannot here be invoked; and if the term 'evolution' be applicable at all to the whole world-process, it must have a different meaning from that which it bears in Darwinian biology. Presumably the world is comparable with a single throw of dice. And common sense is not foolish in suspecting the dice to have been loaded" (*Philosophical Theology*, 2 vols. [London: Cambridge University Press, 1935], 2:87).

16. A popular expression of this doubt, which synthesizes a number of scientific conclusions, may be found in Arthur Koestler's *The Ghost in the Machine* (New York: Macmillan Co., 1967).

17. *Vorlesungen über die Beweise vom Dasein Gottes* (Berlin, 1966), p. 170; translated in *Lectures on the Philosophy of Religion*, trans. E. B. Speirs and Burdon Sanderson, 3 vols. (London: Kegan Paul, Trench, & Trübner, 1895), 3:344.

18. *Critique of Judgment*, n. 86, trans. James Merideth (Oxford: Clarendon Press, 1952), p. 110.

19. *Summa contra gentiles*, bk. I, chap. 13. Translation by Anton Pegis (Doubleday & Co., 1966), p. 96.

20. *Summa contra gentiles*, bk. I, chap. 42.

21. *Logic and Language*, ed. Antony Flew (Garden City, N.Y.: Doubleday & Co., 1965), p. 201.

22. *Why I Am Not a Christian* (New York: Simon & Schuster, 1957), p. 10.

23. Unpublished lectures, Manuscript VII, C-6-6.

24. Cf. H. H. Price's statement that the traditional proofs are not arguments which "would follow logically from premises which every reasonable man is bound to accept."

25. *The Credibility of Divine Existence*, p. 390. By using the term "credibility" Norman Kemp Smith hoped to emphasize that he was not advancing one more argument for the existence of God, but rather an inquiry into the source and status of belief. Cf. introduction, p. 45.

26. J. J. C. Smart describes it as a "potent instrument in heightening religious emotions" ("The Existence of God," in *New Essays in Philosophical Theology*, ed. Antony Flew and Alasdair MacIntyre [New York: Macmillan Co., 1968], p. 45).

# 9
# The Moral and the Ontological Arguments

*The Moral Argument*

In the *Critique of Judgment* Kant had declared the moral will to be the purpose of the world, thus subordinating teleology to morality. But in his final notes, published in the *Opus Posthumum*, morality is increasingly emphasized as a source of religious inspiration. Some passages clearly contradict all that Kant wrote on the autonomy of the moral law in the *Critique of Practical Reason* and anticipate what was to become the moral argument. Thus he maintains that the religious interpretation of all duties is not an addition subsequent to their perception as duties but is immediately and necessarily given with it. This means, as Kemp Smith points out, that "the categorical imperative leads directly to God and affords surety of his reality."[1] "The categorical imperative of the command of duty is grounded in the idea of an *imperantis*, who is all-powerful and holds universal sway. This is the Idea of God."[2]

The idea that conscience is the voice of God was fully developed in Newman's *Grammar of Assent*. Conscience for Newman means much more than moral sense. It is an authoritative "dictate" which threatens and promises, rewards and chastises. Responsibility, fear and shame, all remind us "that there is One to whom we are responsible, before whom we are ashamed, whose claims upon us we fear."[3] The religious impact of the moral imperative is a direct experience open to all men whose religious sense has not been blunted.[4]

An obvious objection to Newman's voice of conscience is that it is conditioned by a religious education. Newman himself

166

requires that the child must have been "safe from influences destructive of his religious instinct."[5] Without positive religious indoctrination a man will rarely find religious meaning in moral precepts. This certainly weakens it as an argument for the existence of God.[6] Yet we need not go into those educational matters to reopen the basic question: Does the moral obligation as such *require* a transcendent Lawgiver? Must the moral imperative be recognized as the voice of God? Does morality need a religious foundation? A reflection upon the moral experience of our contemporaries no longer justifies an unqualifiedly affirmative answer to those questions. Undoubtedly, in our own cultural past most moral heroes were to some extent religiously inspired. But this proves only that the religious attitude has an impact upon man's moral behavior wherever it is adopted. Today such an adoption can no longer be taken for granted. We find as many secular heroes as religious saints. For them at least the moral imperative is not the voice of a transcendent Being. The moral law unquestionably transcends the empirical world: more than science and philosophy it lifts man above the closed world of ordinary experience. But is moral transcendence religious transcendence? The believer himself would be the first to deny that. Karl Jaspers distinguishes clearly the two forms of transcendence:

Although in conscience I am confronted with transcendence, I do not hear the transcendent or listen to it as to a voice from another world. The voice of conscience is not God's voice. In the voice of conscience the Deity remains silent. Here as everywhere God remains hidden. In conscience I see myself referred to transcendence, but I am still centered upon myself. God has not taken away my freedom and my responsibility by manifesting Himself.[7]

Yet, there may be another way of looking at Newman's "argument." He himself did not regard it as a universal proof and believed it to be convincing only if one already possessed a developed notion of God. Moreover, in his *Apologia* he declared himself unable to work out a metaphysical proof for the existence of God, or even to answer the objections against the existing ones. If a metaphysical proof could be made on the basis of conscience, Newman certainly did not feel competent to make it. What he gave, instead, is a personal reflection on the *religious* aspect of morality wherever it is present.[8] Such a reflection cannot produce more than personal evidence for the existence of God. If Newman had been asked to justify his faith in a more universal way, he would have recurred to the classical "ways," while admitting that they are not absolutely conclusive.[9] His own argument convinces only religious man: it achieves no transition from the moral to the religious sphere. Newman reflects on an experience which to the believer is from the beginning both moral *and* religious. The religious believer perceives God immediately in the moral sphere, as we all perceive physical realities directly through impressions upon the sense organs.[10] For him the emotional experience of moral values such as remorse, shame or satisfaction, is accompanied by the awareness of divine approval or disapproval.

Faith, then, perceives an aspect in the moral imperative which makes it intrinsically religious. For religious man God provides a divine sanction, an added dimension, to a self-discovered morality. To hold a religious view of ethics, then, means to consider man's potential for moral development as well as his obligation to realize that potential as God-given without ever declining one's own moral responsibility. Such a view places the moral obligation in a different perspective and thereby adds new weight to it. It also emphasizes the element of otherness which seems to be inherent in the moral imperative. In Newman the considerations on the religious nature of the moral experience are limited to the conscience of religious man. If they are taken to be an "argument" for the existence of God, the crucial transition occurs from the religious experience (implicit in some people's emotional awareness of moral values) to the existence of God.[11] This reduces the moral "proof" to one of religious experience with this difference that it concentrates on an aspect of life which religious man shares with many who do not regard themselves as religious. The common ground gives it a more universal appearance. Yet its probative value can never exceed that of the argument of the religious experience itself to which we shall now direct our attention.

## The Religious Experience

The religious attitude is a unique form of self-transcendence in which man actually names the transcendent on the basis of his alleged communication with it. No succinct definition can describe this experience, because it is not a simple, univocal act but a highly complex, dialectical movement. Religious objects differ in almost every instance; the movement alone remains the same.[12] Assuming, then, that religious experiences differ from other experiences, what do they prove?

It has been argued that the religious experience is directly aware of the presence of a transcendent to which religious faiths attempt to give a specific and rationally coherent content.[13] If this means that man has an idea of the transcendent for which he can account in no other way than by a direct experience of God's existence, the argument is a more religious variation of Descartes' first proof in the *Meditations*.[14] As a "proof" I find this unacceptable for two reasons. One, the direct awareness of the sacred which the argument presupposes to be a common experience, is inaccessible to the majority of men today (even the religious believers). Two, even if a direct experience of the sacred were more common, we still would not be justified in deriving the existence of God from it. The experience of the sacred allows for a number of interpretations, even after the purely psychological and subjectivist ones have been ruled out.

Perhaps the argument can be strengthened by a more careful presentation such as the one Max Scheler provides in *On the Eternal in Man*. According to Scheler the religious act intends God as *really* and *transcendently* existing. Now, since the religious act is an irreducible reality and since this act depends on a really existing transcendent terminus, God must exist.

Only a real being with the essential character of the Divinity can be the cause of man's religious propensity, that is, the propensity to execute in a real sense acts of that class whose acts, though finite experience cannot fulfill them, nevertheless demand fulfillment. The object of religious acts is at the same time the cause of their existence. In other words, all knowledge of God is necessarily knowledge from God.[15]

Mark well, Scheler does not argue that man's religious aspirations must be fulfilled by a religious reality. What he says is that the reality of the aspirations themselves requires a transcendent reality. Not to accept the reality of the terminus is to declare the aspirations themselves illusionary and, ultimately, to lapse back into some reductionist interpretation of the religious experience.

Whatever merit there may be in this way of reasoning, it will never do as an "argument," that is, a reasoning process that is equally convincing to religious and nonreligious man. The religious act unquestionably intends its objects as really existing, but the transition from the existence of the intentional terminus *in the act* to its reality *beyond the act* cannot be made outside the religious consciousness. A comparison with the act of perceiving may illustrate this point. Every perception intends an object that transcends the act of perception. Nevertheless the analysis of the act alone will never "prove" to an outsider that there must be a reality *beyond* the act. A phenomenological analysis (such as Scheler's) may reveal the existence of a being *of* perception, which is ideally, that is, *intentionally*, present to the act, but it cannot reveal the existence of a being *beyond* perception. Much less can the reality of the transcendent terminus be proven by a consideration of the psychological reality of the act, for the intentional object is no part of the *real* act at all: it is only *ideally* present to it. Therefore, to argue from the religious experience to the existence of God is begging the question. The only existence which can be established from an analysis of the act is that of the experience itself and, indirectly, of the person who enjoys the experience.[16]

Of course, the case appears different to the man who already believes in God. For him the transition from the intended object of the experience to an independent, real existence comes so naturally that he remains unaware of it until he attempts to justify it. This is precisely what he does in the ontological argument which brings into focus the transition from the *idea* of God, immanent in the experience, to his actual *existence*. This process of self-understanding can be extended by further reflection to those experiences in which man is first faced with the idea of the transcendent, the experiences of contingency, of finitude, of purpose and order. But the decisive moment remains the transition from the idea to the transcendent reality. In that sense all arguments for the existence of God are based upon an ontological argument, as Kant claimed albeit for different reasons. Indeed, they should be. For if the "arguments" are *reflections* upon a pre-reflective experience, then the "ontological" reflection must be the basis of all others. We shall first criticize it briefly in its traditional form, that is, as a "proof," and then attempt to capture its deeper meaning.

### The Religious Meaning of the Ontological Argument

Anselm of Canterbury is usually credited with the first methodical reflection upon the process by which the mind establishes a transcendent reality in and through a subjective experience.[17] His way of reasoning is well known. If God is that than which nothing greater can be conceived, then He cannot be a *mere* concept, since a perfect Being conceived as *actually* existing would surpass Him. The perfect Being, then, must necessarily be real, because it exists by its own nature. Variations of the argument appear in Descartes' *Meditations* and in Leibniz's *New Essays Concerning Human Understanding* and *Monadology*. It was thoroughly criticized by Kant but immediately afterwards resurrected by Hegel who built his entire philosophy on it.

Kant's main criticism is equally well known: existence cannot be predicated and, consequently, mere analysis can never educe it from a concept. The transition from idea to existence can be made only by means of empirical evidence. Of course, we may conceive God in such a way that a denial of his existence is contradictory, but this remains a sterile, analytic proposition until we prove by empirical evidence that he actually exists. Kant's critique has been qualified time and again. Thus it has been argued that there is *per se* nothing wrong with attributing a real mode of existence to a subject which has only a mental mode of existence, as long as one recognizes the restrictions which the mode of existence of the subject places on that of the predicates.[18] The ontological argument violates those restrictions. The mental existence of the perfect Being allows no conclusions about its real existence. Adding the note "existence" does not change the purely mental status of the subject, as long as no basis is provided for distinguishing a real from an imagined existence. I can always imagine an object as existent, even when I am certain that it does not exist. The notion of God in the ontological argument is taken entirely from nonexistential sources and can, therefore, never move into the realm of reality.

A second basic criticism of the ontological argument is that it fails to clarify whether the notion of perfect Being is in any way meaningful. There is only one way to decide that issue definitively: to prove that such a Being exists. But if that were proven we would need no argument. It is far from self-evident that absolute perfection is a valid concept. That is why Leibniz first set out to prove its possibility. The major premise of his ontological argument is more cautiously stated than that of Descartes. Leibniz admits the necessary existence of God *only* after the notion of God has been proven to be possible. Unfortunately his exceedingly brief proof merely states that nothing can interfere with the possibility of that "which involves no limits, no negation and consequently no contradiction."[19] Leibniz actually presupposes Spinoza's more extensive treatment of the matter in his *Ethics*, where he proves that there is nothing in or outside God that could make him impossible, and if he is possible, he exists.

> If, then, no cause or reason can be given, which prevents the existence of God, or which destroys his existence, we must certainly conclude that he necessarily does exist. If such a reason or cause should be given, it must either be drawn from the very nature of God, or be external to him—that is, drawn from another substance of another nature. For if it were of the same nature, God, by that very fact, would be admitted to exist. But substance of another nature could have nothing in common with God (by prop. 2), and therefore would be unable either to cause or to destroy his existence.[20]

But the absence of logical contradictions provides no information about the *real* possibility of a being, the possibility *quoad se*. The connection of all real properties in one being is a synthesis, and only some actual experience could ever determine whether such a synthesis is possible or not. We may conclude with Kant: "And thus the celebrated Leibniz is far from having succeeded in what he plumed himself on achieving—the comprehension *a priori* of the possibility of this sublime ideal being."[21]

In spite of these formidable objections the ontological argument has always had its defenders. Among the most recent ones are Norman Malcolm and Claude Bruaire.[22] But the main protagonist of the ontological argument in modern times is Hegel whose entire philosophy may be described as a transition from the ideal to the real. In his *Lectures on the Philosophy of Religion* he repeatedly defends the argument against its critics. The notion of God is not merely a subjective idea: it starts as purely ideal, but by its own internal dialectic surpasses this merely ideal stage.[23] Hegel's only objection to Anselm is that he *presupposes* the identity of the notion and reality instead of proving it. Modern man has become too much aware of the subjective nature of thought to take its objective reality for granted: he will accept this reality only after a philosophical study of the notion.[24]

Interestingly enough, those recent revivals of the ontological argument replace the notion in the religious consciousness from which Anselm took it.[25] The new viewpoint differs from that of Descartes,[26] Spinoza, and Leibniz who pretended to build up an argument by logical reasoning alone. Kant's objections retain their full force against the logical process, but become powerless against a rational reflection upon the religious act. Nor is this religious meaning extrinsic to the argument. It was, I believe, its original meaning. Anselm attempted to attain a deeper understanding of his faith, not to generate faith or to prove it. His argument, presented in the form of a prayer, clearly gives the precedence to faith over understanding. *Credo ut intelligam*. Faith comes first, but once it is present, it requires a justification by reason.

The ontological argument, in this perspective, is ultimately the logical explication of the religious experience. It is not in the notion of God that the transition to a divine reality occurs, but in the experience which supports the notion. Whatever positive content the notion of a perfect Being may have it takes from a specific religious experience. Just as Newman's moral argument merely articulates the experience of the man who understands the dictates of conscience as divine commands and thereby already relates his moral self to a transcendent Being, so the ontological argument merely explicates what was implicitly present in the believer's self-transcending experience. Such a reflection on experience is no "argument" at all, for it provides no new information on the ontological status of the idea of God. William Ernest Hocking therefore reformulates the ontological "argument" from "I have an idea of God, therefore God exists," to "I have an idea of God, therefore I have an experience of God."[27] Idea and experience are given simultaneously, since the idea is no other than the experience recognized.[28] Of course, such reasoning does not apply to all ideas: some are merely tentative sketches for providing logical structure to experience. But those basic and irreducible ideas which define an entire area of experience are given with the experience. Such an idea, I would claim with Hocking, is the idea of God to most religious men in an advanced culture. Yet to separate the idea from the actual experience and then to expect that it will be a valid substitute to those who lack the latter, can only give rise to the logical fallacy known as the ontological argument. A similar fallacy results when the individual experience is used as a universal "logical argument" to define the ontological status of the object *independently* of the actual experience. Experience never proves any other than its own existence and that of its intentional terminus *to the extent that it is immanent* in the experience.

If correctly presented the ontological argument shows that the notion of God is not a mere logical construction, but the expression of a fundamental experience of self-transcendence. Only its origin in experience makes the idea of God worthy of being logically explored. This is what the other arguments attempt to do: they bring out the coherent character of the idea of God by relating it to other, more mundane experiences. The ontological argument alone cannot fulfill this function, for its nature is exclusively religious. That is why it has found little favor among those who consider the other "ways" to be valid arguments.

The arguments are religious not only in origin but also in nature. They describe precisely those experiences in which the mind is confronted with the problem of transcendence. They rationally analyze what religious man does when he transcends the empirical in the religious sphere. They justify this transcendence as far as reason can justify it. But by themselves they do not *prove* God's existence, since they do not pass beyond the point where the nature of the transcendent becomes a real problem and where the religious answer (including the existence of God) must be envisaged as a *possible* solution.

## NOTES

1. *A Commentary to Kant's Critique of Pure Reason*, 2d Edition, p. 638.

2. Erich Adickes, *Kants Opus Posthumum* (Berlin, 1920), p. 108. The change does not necessarily imply a purer religious view of morality for it seems to be accompanied by a more immanent interpretation of God. "God must be represented not as substance outside me, but as the highest moral principle in me." *Ibid.*, p. 374. Some would argue that the religious foundation of the moral imperative was already implied in Kant's published writings. Referring to the latter W. E. Hocking wrote: "Kant was dead-right in finding a sense of obligation at the center of our consciousness: there's an aboriginal I-ought which goes with I-exist. . . . The only point is, there is no obligation which is not an obligation *to* some living self, other than myself. The I-ought implies a Thou-art, coextensive with the world I am bound to think. That Thou is the self within the world, the one elemental Other. Its common name is God. Kant was very close to seeing that, only he seemed to assume that an I-ought could stand by itself, and support God, whereas God is simply the rest of the ought's being." (Letter of October 14, 1954, to Prof. P. H. Epps of the University of North Carolina.)

3. *A Grammar of Assent* (New York: Doubleday, 1958), p. 101.

4. Some present it as a more reflective process. For Jacques Maritain, for instance, when a person realizes that something ought to be done *because it is good* or omitted *because it is evil*, he wholly transcends the empirical order: he begins to understand that the law ruling human activity depends on a reality which is good by virtue of itself, not by its conformity to something else. *The Range of Reason* (New York: Scribner, 1952), p. 69. Others see in the moral obligation evidence of man's contingency, and thus reduce the whole proof to the "third way." See, P. Descoqs, *Praelectiones Theologiae Naturalis* (Rome, 1932), Vol. I, pp. 463-68.

5. *Op. cit.*, p. 103.

6. Antony Flew, *God and Philosophy* (New York: Harcourt, Brace, 1966), p. 113.

7. *Philosophie* (Berlin: Springer, 1932), Vol. 2, p. 272.

8. J. H. Walgrave, *Newman the Theologian* (New York: Sheed and Ward, 1960), p. 362.

9. J. H. Walgrave, *op. cit.*, p. 207.

10. J. H. Newman, *A Grammar of Assent*, p. 102. A similar view is expressed by W. E. Hocking in "Science in Its Relation to Value," in *The Rice Institute Pamphlet*, 29 (1942), p. 221.

11. One unpublished passage brings this out clearly: "If then our or my knowledge of our or my experience is brought home to me by my consciousness of thinking, and if thinking includes as one of its modes conscience or the sense of an imperative coercive law, and if such a sense (when analyzed, i.e., reflected on) invokes an inchoative recognition of a Divine Being, it follows that such recognition comes close upon my recognition that I am. . . ." *Unpublished Philosophical Writings called "Sundries,"* quoted in A. J. Boekraad, *The Personal Conquest of Truth According to J. H. Newman* (Louvain, 1955), p. 266, Note.

12. I have developed the dialectical nature of the religious experience in *The Other Dimension* (Doubleday, 1972).

13. Norman Kemp Smith, *The Credibility of Divine Existence* (New York: St. Martin's Press, 1967), pp. 393-96.

14. "But, among these my ideas . . . there is one that represents a God. . . . And thus it is absolutely necessary to conclude from all that I have before said, that God exists: for though the idea of substance be in my mind owing to this, that I myself am a substance, I should not, however, have the idea of an infinite substance, seeing I am a finite being, unless it were given me by some substance in reality infinite." *Oeuvres de Descartes*, ed. Adam-Tannery (Paris, 1897-1913), pp. 44-45; transl. John Veitch in *The Rationalists*, pp. 135, 137.

15. *On the Eternal in Man*, transl. Bernard Noble (New York: Harper, 1960), p. 261.

16. See T. MacPherson, *The Philosophy of Religion* (Princeton: Van Nostrand, 1965), p. 122.

17. Anselm, *Opera*, Migne 158, pp. 223-42. Transl. *The Proslogium*, A. N. Deane (Chicago, 1910). Augustine anticipates Anselm's reasoning in the *Confessions*, VII, 6, but, in typical Neo-Platonic fashion, he establishes that the God whom he adores is the supreme Good, rather than the supreme Being.

18. See William Alston, "The Ontological Argument Revisited," *The Philosophical Review*, 69 (1960), pp. 452-74.

19. *Die philosophischen Schriften von G. W. Leibniz*, ed. C. I. Gerhardt (Berlin, 1875-1890), Vol. VI, p. 614. *The Monadology*, p. 45, transl. George Montgomery-Albert Chandler, in *The Rationalists*, p. 462.

20. *Ethica* in *Benedicti de Spinoza Opera*, ed. Van Vloten and Land

(The Hague: Martinus Nijhoff, 1882), Bk. I, Prop. 77, p. 461. Transl. R. H. M. Elwes in *The Rationalists*, p. 184. James F. Ross, who analyzes this argument carefully, finds a predecessor of it in John Duns Scotus' *Reportata Parisiensia*, I, d.2, 2.2, n.6, *Philosophical Theology* (Indianapolis: Bobbs-Merrill, 1969), p. 174.

21. *Critique of Pure Reason*, A 602 B 630. Transl. Norman Kemp Smith (New York: St. Martin's Press, 1965), p. 507.

22. For Norman Malcolm's statement and the critique by Alvin Plantinga and Paul Hanle, see *The Ontological Argument*, ed. Alvin Plantinga (New York: Doubleday, 1965), pp. 136-180. Claude Bruaire reasons, somewhat in the tradition of Blondel, from the idea of infinite perfection which is at the origin of all human striving to the real existence of an absolute, free being. *L'affirmation de Dieu* (Paris, 1964), pp. 163-68.

23. See *Vorlesungen über die Philosophie der Religion*, ed. Georg Lasson (Hamburg: Meiner, 1966), Vol. I, p. 50.

24. *Vorlesungen über die Beweise vom Dasein Gottes* (Hamburg: Meiner, 1966), Appendix, p. 175. Transl. "Amplification of the Ontological Proof in the Lectures on the Philosophy of Religion for the Year 1831," by E. B. Speirs and J. B. Sanderson in *Lectures on the Philosophy of Religion*, Vol. III, pp. 360-67.

25. This is obvious for Bruaire, Malcolm, and Hartshorne, less so for Hegel whose religious consciousness is "surpassed" by the philosophical one, but who nevertheless explicitly refers to the religious *source* of the ontological concept. A qualifiedly religious interpretation of the notion of "necessary being" in Anselm is also given by John Hick, "God As Necessary Being," in *The Journal of Philosophy*, 57 (1960), pp. 729-30.

26. The status of the ontological argument in Descartes is somewhat uncertain, for unless one admits that there is an obvious circle (he needs the conclusion of an argument for the existence of God to make his idea of God sufficiently reliable), it would seem that Descartes is more interested in establishing the ultimate rational foundation of the preceding two proofs than in construing a new argument. A.M. Guéroult, *Nouvelles réflexions sur la preuve ontologique de Descartes* (Paris, 1955).

27. *The Meaning of God in Human Experience* (New Haven: Yale University Press, 1963), p. 314.

28. *Ibid.*, p. 568. For a discussion of Hocking's ontological "argument," cf. Mary Giegengack, "The Role of Experience in Man's Knowledge of God According to William E. Hocking's Philosophy of Religion" (Unpublished Ph.D. Dissertation, Georgetown University, 1971).